THE ULTIMATE BASEBALL TRIVIA CHALLENGE

OVER 600 QUIZ QUESTIONS FOR
DIE-HARD BASEBALL FANS

HANK PATTON

ISBN: 979-8-89095-047-5

Copyright © 2024 by Curious Press

ALL RIGHTS RESERVED

No part of this book may be reproduced, stored in a retrieval system, or transmitted in any form or by any means, electronic, mechanical, photocopying, recording, scanning, or otherwise, without the prior written permission of the publisher.

CONTENTS

INTRODUCTION 1
CHAPTER 1: THE ORIGINS OF THE GAME 4
    Chapter 1 Answers 8
    Did You Know? 9
CHAPTER 2: THE EARLY DAYS 11
    Chapter 2 Answers 14
    Did You Know? 15
CHAPTER 3: THE BEST OF THE REST 17
    Chapter 3 Answers 20
    Did You Know? 20
CHAPTER 4: 1900 TO 1915 22
    Chapter 4 Answers 26
    Did You Know? 27
CHAPTER 5: 1916 TO 1930 29
    Chapter 5 Answers 33
    Did You Know? 33
CHAPTER 6: THE 1930S 35
    Chapter 6 Answers 38
    Did You Know? 38
CHAPTER 7: THE 1940S 40
    Chapter 7 Answers 43
    Did You Know? 43
CHAPTER 8: THE 1950S 45

    Chapter 8 Answers 48
    Did You Know? 48
CHAPTER 9: THE 1960S 50
    Chapter 9 Answers 53
    Did You Know? 53
CHAPTER 10: THE 1970S 55
    Chapter 10 Answers 58
    Did You Know? 58
CHAPTER 11: THE 1980S 60
    Chapter 11 Answers 63
    Did You Know? 63
CHAPTER 12: THE 1990S 65
    Chapter 12 Answers 68
    Did You Know? 68
CHAPTER 13: THE 2000S 70
    Chapter 13 Answers 73
    Did You Know? 73
CHAPTER 14: THE 2010S 75
    Chapter 14 Answers 78
    Did You Know? 78
CHAPTER 15: TEAMS COMING AND GOING 80
    Chapter 15 Answers 83
    Did You Know? 83
CHAPTER 16: FORMER LEAGUES & DIVISIONS 85
    Chapter 16 Answers 88
    Did You Know? 88
CHAPTER 17: THE AMERICAN LEAGUE 90
    Chapter 17 Answers 93

Did You Know? 93

CHAPTER 18: THE NATIONAL LEAGUE 95
Chapter 18 Answers..99
Did You Know? 99

CHAPTER 19: AL EAST 101
Chapter 19 Answers..105
Did You Know? 105

CHAPTER 20: AL CENTRAL 107
Chapter 20 Answers..111
Did You Know? 111

CHAPTER 21: AL WEST 113
Chapter 21 Answers..117
Did You Know? 117

CHAPTER 22: NL EAST 119
Chapter 22 Answers..123
Did You Know? 123

CHAPTER 23: NL CENTRAL 125
Chapter 23 Answers..129
Did You Know? 129

CHAPTER 24: NL WEST 131
Chapter 24 Answers..135
Did You Know? 135

CHAPTER 25: THE WORLD SERIES 137
Chapter 25 Answers..141
Did You Know? 141

CHAPTER 26: BASEBALL HALL OF FAME 143
Chapter 26 Answers..146
Did You Know? 146

CHAPTER 27: HOME RUN KINGS 148
Chapter 27 Answers 151
Did You Know? 151

CHAPTER 28: GOLDEN GLOVES 153
Chapter 28 Answers 156
Did You Know? 156

CHAPTER 29: CY YOUNG AWARD WINNERS 158
Chapter 29 AnswerS 161
Did You Know? 161

CHAPTER 30: UNBEATABLE RECORDS 163
Chapter 30 Answers 166
Did You Know? 166

CHAPTER 31: THE BIGGEST MOMENTS 168
Chapter 31 Answers 171
Did You Know? 171

CHAPTER 32: THE ALL-STAR GAME 173
Chapter 32 Answers 176
Did You Know? 176

CHAPTER 33: SCANDALS & HEADLINES 178
Chapter 33 Answers 181
Did You Know? 181

CHAPTER 34: STATISTICS & ACRONYMS 183
Chapter 34 Answers 184
Did You Know? 184

CONCLUSION 185

ATTENTION:

DO YOU WANT MY FUTURE BOOKS AT HEAVY DISCOUNTS AND EVEN FOR FREE?

HEAD OVER TO WWW.SECRETREADS.COM

AND JOIN MY SECRET BOOK CLUB!

INTRODUCTION

The greatest thing about the sport of baseball is its multi-storied history. Teams, players, and managers have accomplished the unthinkable and the impossible over the more than 100 years that it has been played. It's been a celebrated tradition for a significant portion of the history of this young country.

For people like you, the fans of the game, there is plenty to explore and learn about the game's past. There are records being broken all the time, but knowing how those records came to be is just as important. You learn the game's history so you can better understand the importance of milestones set today and those set in the future.

This book is designed to test your knowledge of the history of the game. Every aspect of the sport is covered, and all the league's teams feature in these questions. Do you remember a team's past and present, where they were founded, and where they ended up? Can you remember the top players of years gone by?

After all, the game has changed over time. Technology has improved, making an impact on equipment and player training, so today's game looks much different than it did in the past. Still, players back then did what they had to do to find success, and their contributions to the lore of the sport should be celebrated and remembered.

Each chapter will cover one topic or theme, so be sure to visit each one and test your skills. Even the biggest fans will likely find there are some gaps in their knowledge of this great sport. Everyone has heard of the big home run hitters and the great pitchers of the day, but there are tons of players who have accomplished amazing feats.

There are plenty of challenges to be found within these pages, along with some facts you may not have known before. So, if you're ready, gather your group of baseball friends and see who knows the most about one of the top sports in the world.

It's a book full of fun, and you're sure to learn something new. Step up to the plate and take your best swing at the fastball coming your way!

CHAPTER 1:
THE ORIGINS OF THE GAME

1. The game of baseball evolved as a variation of what popular sport from England?
   A. Cricket
   B. Rounders
   C. Town ball
   D. Tennis

2. William Wheaton was a founding member of which baseball group in 1845?
   A. The Gotham Club
   B. The Knickerbocker Base Ball Club
   C. The Eagle Club
   D. The Union Club

3. Which of these rules was not accurate in the baseball of the 1840s?
   A. Pitchers must pitch the ball underhand.
   B. A foul ball is not a strike.
   C. The first team to 21 runs (or aces) wins.
   D. Catching a fair ball on the first bounce is not an out.

4. Which of these years was the first to see a New York journalist call baseball America's "national pastime"?
   A. 1851
   B. 1852
   C. 1856
   D. 1858

5. How many teams comprised the National Association of Base Ball Players in 1857?
   A. 10
   B. 12
   C. 14

D. 16

6. The children's publication called A Little Pretty Pocket-Book, which contained the earliest known mention of baseball, was published in which year?

   A. 1822
   B. 1744
   C. 1758
   D. 1810

7. The first description of a baseball game in a U.S. news publication, was printed on September 10, 1845, by which publication?

   A. The New York Times
   B. The New York Post
   C. The New York Morning News
   D. The New York Daily

8. The first known box score ever published featured New York and Brooklyn Clubs playing where?

   A. Hoboken, New Jersey
   B. Manhattan, New York
   C. Staten Island, New York
   D. Philadelphia, Pennsylvania

9. The first American law prohibiting baseball appeared in what year?

   A. 1799
   B. 1791
   C. 1822
   D. 1803

10. The first All-Star game took place in which year, the same year that first featured the called strike rule?

    A. 1856
    B. 1857
    C. 1858
    D. 1859

11. Two clubs formed in 1859, and one of them survives to this day. Which modern team is it?

A. Toronto Blue Jays
   B. Detroit Tigers
   C. Atlanta Braves
   D. Washington Nationals

12. The first time a distance for a pitcher to be standing from the batter was established was in 1854, at what distance?

    A. "Not less than 20 paces"
    B. "Not less than 15 paces"
    C. "Not less than ten paces"
    D. "Not less than five paces"

13. In 1869, which team became the first established as a fully professional team?

    A. Cincinnati Red Stockings
    B. Chicago White Stockings
    C. New York Yankees
    D. New York Mets

14. Which of these choices best describes how many teams were in the National Association of Base Ball Players after ten years of existence?

    A. Over 100
    B. Over 200
    C. Over 300
    D. Over 400

15. What historical event helped the growth of baseball, as many came together to play it?

    A. The War of 1812
    B. The Civil War
    C. The Mexican American War
    D. The American Revolution

16. The first-ever game between the "New York Nine" and the New York Knickerbockers ended with which lopsided score?

    A. 10-0
    B. 17-3
    C. 23-1
    D. 12-2

17. Infamously, Black players were banned from the NABBP during which year?

   A. 1867
   B. 1863
   C. 1880
   D. 1871

18. In 1863, the NABBP decided that catching a fair ball after one bounce wouldn't count as what?

   A. A double
   B. An out
   C. A single
   D. A balk

CHAPTER 1 ANSWERS:

1. B. Rounders. There was much debate in the 1800s about the origins of baseball, but history proved that it was a regional version of rounders.
2. B. The Knickerbocker Base Ball Group. Wheaton also helped the Gotham Club write their rules, though he was not a founding member.
3. D. Catching the ball on the first bounce is not an out. In early baseball, it was considered an out if a fielder caught the ball after the first bounce.
4. C. 1856. The journalists in New York were also calling it the "national game."
5. D. 16, and they quickly changed that rule regarding the one-bounce out.
6. B. 1744, but it depicted posts instead of bases.
7. C. The New York Morning News.
8. A. Hoboken, New Jersey. New York beat Brooklyn 24-4.
9. B. 1791. Pittsfield, Massachusetts created a town bylaw preventing the game from being played near the town's meeting house.
10. C. 1858. It was also the first year that games were charging admission for spectators.
11. D. Washington Nationals. The National club formed in November of 1859 in Washington D.C., and although it has gone through many changes, the Nationals are still in the city today.
12. B. "Not less than 15 paces." It was agreed upon by three different clubs, The Knickerbocker Club, Eagle Club, and Gotham Club.
13. A. Cincinnati Red Stockings. They went undefeated against semiprofessional teams and amateur teams that year.
14. D. Over 400. Despite the numbers, the strongest teams were in the northeast United States.
15. B. The Civil War. Troops from the north would play together while in camp between battles.
16. C. 23-1. It only took four innings, too.
17. A. 1867. It was a decision that would affect baseball history for nearly a century.
18. B. An out. As players got better at hitting, it only made sense.

DID YOU KNOW?

The NABBP began to splinter after the formation of the first professional teams, and the organization would fold a few years later.

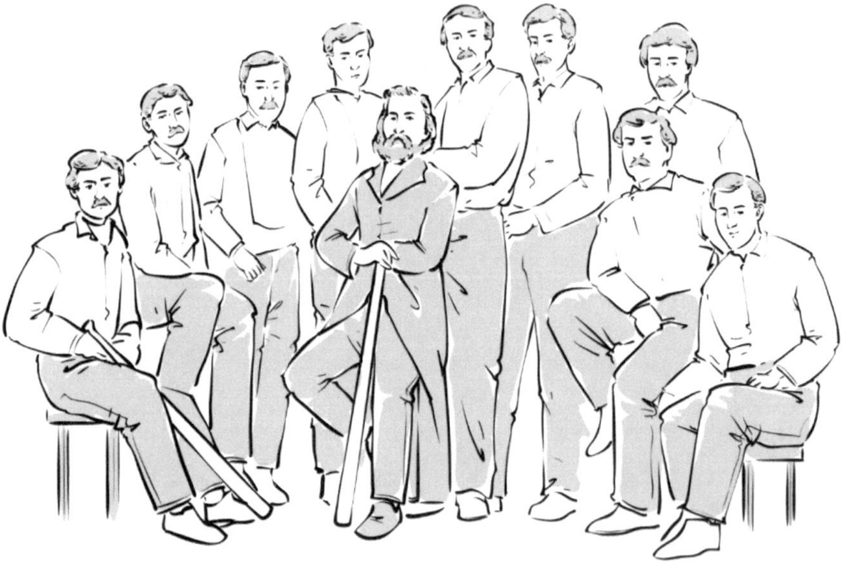

CHAPTER 2:
THE EARLY DAYS

1. Aside from the National Association of Professional Base Ball Players' attempt, what was the first professional league in baseball?

    A. American League
    B. National League
    C. Union League
    D. Western League

2. True or False: The NAPBBP has had eight former players inducted into the Baseball Hall of Fame, either as players or executives.

3. Which NAPBBP player is credited with inventing the curveball?

    A. Pud Galvin
    B. Candy Cummings
    C. Deacon White
    D. Jim O'Rourke

4. True or False: The NAPBBP would rank teams in the standings by games won, rather than win percentage, even when teams didn't play an equal number of games.

5. For the five years of NAPBBP play, Lip Pike led the league in home runs. How many did he hit in those five seasons?

    A. 73
    B. 11
    C. 29
    D. 16

6. How many teams made the jump from the NAPBBP to the National League in 1876?

    A. Four
    B. Five
    C. Six
    D. Ten

7. One of the reasons the NAPBBP struggled was due to one team being dominant. Which team was it?

   A. Philadelphia Athletics
   B. Chicago White Stockings
   C. Boston Red Stockings
   D. Washington Olympics

8. Which of these players led the 1871 NAPBBP season in both RBIs (runs batted in) and OBA (opponents' batting average)?

   A. Rynie Wolters
   B. Albert Spalding
   C. Al Pratt
   D. George Zettlein

9. Ivers Whitney Adams founded the Boston Base Ball Club and the Boston Red Stockings in January of 1871 for how much money?

   A. $500
   B. $1,200
   C. $7,000
   D. $15,000

10. Umpire Mort Rogers made a scorecard with a picture of Harry Wright, center fielder for the Red Stockings, on the front. Many consider this to be a version of the first what?

    A. Ticket stubs
    B. Game programs
    C. Baseball cards
    D. Roster books

11. True or False: In a June game between the Troy Haymakers and the Fort Wayne Kekiongas, the Fort Wayne team protested a replacement ball in the first inning because of cheating rumors.

12. True or False: The New York Mutuals lost their stadium in an 1871 fire that ravaged the city.

13. In one infamous game, the Chicago White Stockings lost 38-1 against the New York Mutuals. The Mutuals had 33 hits, but Chicago had 36 what?

    A. Errors
    B. Hits

C. Strikeouts
D. Steals

14. In 1876, the first year of the new National League, which team finished in last place, only winning nine games out of 65?

    A. Louisville Grays
    B. Cincinnati Reds
    C. St. Louis Brown Stockings
    D. Hartford Dark Blues

15. William Hulbert founded the National League to replace the NAPBBP for many reasons. Which of these is not one of them?

    A. Drunk players
    B. Players corrupted by the gambling community
    C. Teams in small cities
    D. To open side-businesses in stadiums

16. Boston won the first game of the National League when they beat which team?

    A. Chicago White Stockings
    B. Hartford Dark Blues
    C. Philadelphia Athletics
    D. Cincinnati Reds

17. True or False: By 1880, only two of the founding teams remained in the National League.

18. True or False: The New York Mutuals and Philadelphia Athletics were expelled from the league for refusing to play certain teams with players of Irish descent.

CHAPTER 2 ANSWERS:

1. B. National League. It was founded in 1876.
2. True. Four of the players would go on to have significant careers in the National League.
3. B. Candy Cummings. Despite his invention, Cummings was only inducted into the HoF as a pioneer of the game, not for his accomplishments as a player on the field.
4. True. In their five seasons of professional competition, though, the winning team had the most wins and the best winning percentage.
5. D. 16. This was part of the Dead Ball era, when very few home runs were hit.
6. C. Six. There were also two independent teams that joined at the founding of the new league.
7. C. Boston Red Stockings. They won all but one championship during the NAPBBP's existence.
8. A. Rynie Wolters. The other choices in this question each led different pitching categories during the same season.
9. D. $15,000. That is more than $375,000 in modern money.
10. C. Baseball cards. It was an early concept, but the marketing would evolve over time.
11. False. Fort Wayne did protest a replacement ball when the game ball ripped, but it happened in the sixth inning of the game. Fort Wayne forfeited the game.
12. False. It was the Great Chicago Fire of 1871 that destroyed the Chicago White Stockings' stadium.
13. A. Errors. It didn't help that Chicago's pitcher, George Zettlein, was suspended at the time.
14. B. Cincinnati Reds. It's important to note that this team was not related to the Cincinnati Red Stockings from the NAPBBP.
15. D. To open side-businesses in stadiums. He was mostly concerned with the mayhem and corruption, and the baseball world is better for it.
16. C. Philadelphia Athletics. The Athletics were one of two teams that were kicked out of the league after one season.
17. True. Those two teams are still in operation today: Boston and Chicago are now the Atlanta Braves and Chicago Cubs.

18. False. The two teams were expelled for refusing to play western road trips toward the end of the season. They had slipped in the standings and wanted to play amateur teams at home to make up for their financial losses.

DID YOU KNOW?

The NAPBBP's entry fee for teams was only $10.

CHAPTER 3:
THE BEST OF THE REST

1. 1. Harry Wright is credited with implementing which of these techniques?

   A. Pick-off throws
   B. Intentional walks
   C. Defensive alignment shifts
   D. Bunts to advance runners

2. 2. The Boston Red Stockings' final season in the NAPBBP ended with what winning percentage?

   A. .743
   B. .899
   C. .729
   D. .830

3. 3. Ross Barnes led the NAPBBP in both hits and runs with _____ and _____, respectively.

   A. 425, 390
   B. 298, 225
   C. 345, 289
   D. 540, 462

4. 4. Albert Spalding led the NAPBBP in wins as a pitcher before joining the Chicago White Stockings in 1876, but what is his name most known for today?

   A. Sporting goods
   B. Cigarette brand
   C. Baseball hat designs
   D. Baseball uniform overhaul

5. 5. The American Association of Base Ball Clubs (AA), founded in 1882, lasted how many years?

   A. Eight

B. Nine
C. Ten
D. 11

6. 6. The AA differed from the NL in many ways, but which of these was not one of them?

    A. Cheaper tickets
    B. Tuesday games
    C. Sunday games
    D. Alcohol for sale

7. True or False: The AA would often be called "The Beer and Whiskey League" because many of the teams were backed by breweries or distilleries.

8. True or False: The Brooklyn Bridegrooms won the AA league championship, then won the 1889 World Series before switching to the National League, then won the World Series again.

9. 9. The Players' League only lasted for one full season, but they helped build new facilities that went on to be used by National League teams for a long time, including 66 years as which team's home?

    A. New York Yankees
    B. New York Giants
    C. New York Mets
    D. New York Knickerbockers

10. The first team to jump from the AA to the National League in 1887 was which franchise?

    A. Baltimore Orioles
    B. New York Metropolitans
    C. Washington Nationals
    D. Pittsburgh Pirates

11. True or False: The St. Louis Maroons of the Union Association joined the National League and remained there until today, though the team's name has changed.

12. Which is the only team from the American Association to win the World Series over an NL team?

    A. St. Louis Browns

B. Louisville Colonels
C. Brooklyn Bridegrooms
D. Cincinnati Red Stockings

13. True or False: Four former American Association teams have won more than 10,000 games in Major League Baseball.

14. 14.	True or False: The Cleveland Infants was a real baseball team in the Players' League.

15. The American Association also featured the first Black player, Moses Walker. Which position did he play?

    A. Pitcher
    B. Catcher
    C. Shortstop
    D. Center Field

16. The Cleveland Spiders defected from the AA to the National League, but they only survived for how many years there?

    A. 12
    B. 11
    C. Ten
    D. Nine

17. While many negro leagues tried to form before 1900, they all folded. Instead, what did these players try instead?

    A. Playing overseas
    B. Coaching
    C. Barnstorming
    D. Protesting

18. 18.	By the end of the 1800s, there was one modern rule still not in effect. What was it?

    A. Pitching overhand
    B. Foul balls count as strikes
    C. Distance to the mound
    D. Sliding into home plate

CHAPTER 3 ANSWERS:

1. C. Defensive alignment shifts. His ideas were critical to bringing down rampant scoring in baseball.
2. B. .899. The Red Stockings won 71 games, lost eight, and tied three during the 1875 season.
3. D. 540, 462. It was a high-scoring league!
4. A. Sporting goods. Spalding is a popular brand of sports equipment founded by Albert Spalding himself.
5. C. Ten. It had 25 different teams over those ten years, with a peak of 12 teams for a single season.
6. C. Sunday games. The NL thought the AA represented cities with lower morality and social standards.
7. True. The nickname came from NL owners that disapproved, but it was still marketable.
8. True. It represented the trouble that the AA had with keeping teams in their league.
9. B. New York Giants. Brotherhood Park was used for 75 years for various sporting events.
10. D. Pittsburgh Pirates. They were known as the Pittsburgh Allegheny's back then, though.
11. False. The team did reach the National League, but they only lasted five seasons there before they folded.
12. A. St. Louis Browns. They defeated Chicago 4-2.
13. True. The Pittsburgh Pirates, Cincinnati Reds, Los Angeles Dodgers, and the St. Louis Cardinals have all accomplished the feat.
14. True. They finished seventh out of eight teams during the 1890 season and folded, as did the league, at the end of the year.
15. B. Catcher. Walker played one year for the Toledo Blue Stockings.
16. B. 11. The team captured one Temple Cup in 1895.
17. C. Barnstorming. It is the act of traveling to small towns to put on exhibition matches. Much like the Harlem Globetrotters of today.
18. B. Foul balls count as strikes. That rule would not be implemented until 1901.

DID YOU KNOW?

At the turn of the century, the American League was only one year away from its formation.

CHAPTER 4:
1900 TO 1915

1. The American League was in business from 1885, but only changed its name to American League in 1900. What was its previous name?

    A. Union League
    B. Great Lakes League
    C. Players' League
    D. Western League

2. In the 1901 season, Cy Young of which team led the American League in wins, ERA, and strikeouts?

    A. Detroit Tigers
    B. Boston Americans
    C. Baltimore Orioles
    D. Cleveland Bluebirds

3. On June 2, 1902, the Cleveland Bronchos committed the most errors in a single inning by any team in the 20th century. How many did they commit?

    A. Four
    B. Five
    C. Six
    D. Seven

4. True or False: On July 8, 1902, Philadelphia Athletics' Danny Murphy arrived late to a game against Boston, entering near the end of the second inning, then went 6-for-6 with a grand slam against Cy Young.

5. In the first modern World Series, which took place in 1903, the Boston Americans defeated the Pittsburgh Pirates in a series that lasted how many games?

    A. Four
    B. Five

C. Seven
D. Eight

6. In a record that will likely never be matched, Cy Young threw how many consecutive hitless innings over a four-game stretch?

   A. 20
   B. 23
   C. 25
   D. 28

7. The 1905 World Series was the first to be a best-of-seven contest, with which team triumphing over the Philadelphia Athletics?

   A. New York Giants
   B. Pittsburgh Pirates
   C. Chicago Cubs
   D. Philadelphia Phillies

8. Tom Hughes of the Washington Senators became the first pitcher to pitch a shutout and do what in 1906?

   A. Make an error to lose the game
   B. Steal home plate to score the only run
   C. Hit a home run as the only run scored in the game
   D. Leave the game with an injury and then return to win

9. True or False: Game 1 of the 1907 World Series was declared a tie because of a bad storm.

10. True or False: The 1908 song, "Take Me Out to the Ball Game," was created by two men who had never attended a baseball game before.

11. Which of these teams became the first to lose three straight World Series in 1909?

    A. Pittsburgh Pirates
    B. Philadelphia Phillies
    C. Detroit Tigers
    D. Boston Red Sox

12. Nap Lajoie wanted to catch Ty Cobbs' score for the league's highest batting average at the end of the 1910 season to win the first-ever Chalmers award, which included a Chalmers Model 30

vehicle as a prize. Though he did not catch Cobb, what did he accomplish on the last day of the season?

   A. He hit three home runs
   B. He bunted for six hits
   C. He went 4-for-4
   D. He hit for the cycle

13. The 1911 World Series suffered a delay of how many days because of constant rain?

    A. Four
    B. Five
    C. Six
    D. Eight

14. The 1912 MLB season featured the first time which ballpark was used?

    A. Fenway Park
    B. Yankee Stadium
    C. Polo Grounds
    D. League Park

15. The Federal League of Base Ball Clubs became a pro league in 1914, creating competition and raising player wages. What did MLB owners call this league?

    A. Loser League
    B. Sellout League
    C. Poor Man's League
    D. Outlaw League

16. True or False: The Philadelphia Athletics became the first team to sweep the World Series in 1914.

17. In 1915, which legendary player hit his first career home run?

    A. Hank Aaron
    B. Babe Ruth
    C. Braggo Roth
    D. Mickey Mantle

18. The 1915 World Series was the last time the Philadelphia Phillies would reach the Series until which year?

A. 1967
B. 1959
C. 1950
D. 1971

CHAPTER 4 ANSWERS:

1. D. Western League. They changed their name in part because of teams removed from the National League.
2. B. Boston Americans. It would be Cy Young's only Triple Crown.
3. C. Six. Those errors were committed against the Baltimore Orioles, who happened to finish at the bottom of the AL that year.
4. True. He also figured in 12 defensive plays without an error.
5. D. It was a 5-3 victory for Boston.
6. B. 23. Those innings included one perfect game that took place on May 5, 1904.
7. A. New York Giants. The Giants finished their season with 105 wins, 13 more than their World Series opponent.
8. C. Hit a home run as the only run scored in the game. It was a 1-0 victory that needed ten innings to decide.
9. False. The Cubs and Tigers were in the 12th inning, tied at 3, when the game was declared a draw due to darkness.
10. True. The lyrics of the original are quite different from what is sung today, as there are verses removed.
11. C. Detroit Tigers. They lost Game 7 of the 1909 World Series 8-0.
12. B. He bunted for seven hits. After it was determined that Lajoie had not caught Cobb, Hugh Chalmers decided to give Lajoie a car, anyway.
13. C. Six. The record would be broken in 1989 by the Loma Prieta earthquake, though, incidentally, that Series featured the same two teams as this one (Philadelphia Athletics and New York Giants, now the Oakland Athletics and San Francisco Giants).
14. A. Fenway Park. It was one of three stadiums introduced that year, and it's the only one of those three still in use.
15. D. Outlaw League. Though they only lasted two years, they were responsible for building Wrigley Field.
16. False. The Athletics were swept by the Boston Braves, the first team to accomplish the feat.
17. B. Babe Ruth. His first home run came on the road against the Yankees, too.
18. C. 1950. The Phillies lost the 1915 World Series 4-1 to the Red Sox.

DID YOU KNOW?

Ty Cobb was not well-liked by baseball fans around the country, partly due to a controversy regarding accusations of violent behavior.

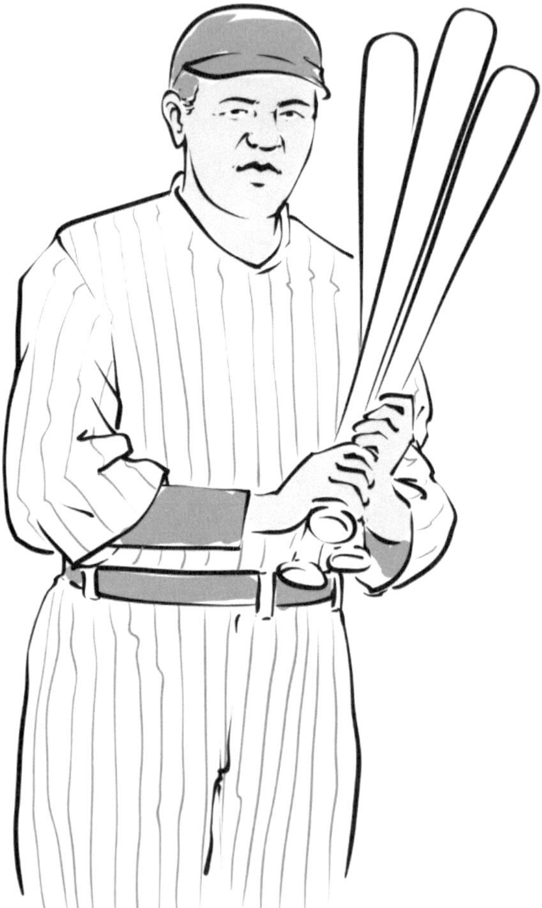

CHAPTER 5:
1916 TO 1930

1. 1. Though not primarily remembered for his pitching, Babe Ruth led the 1916 American League in which of these categories?

    A. Wins
    B. ERA
    C. Strikeouts
    D. Walks

2. 2. In a May 9, 1916, game, the Athletics and Tigers set an MLB record by pitching how many walks between the two teams?

    A. 21
    B. 25
    C. 30
    D. 33

3. 3. The Chicago White Sox won the 1917 World Series, but they wouldn't win it again for how many years?

    A. 56
    B. 64
    C. 79
    D. 88

4. Which player was the first major leaguer to be killed in action during World War I?

    A. Eddie Grant
    B. Alex Burr
    C. Larry Chappell
    D. Ralph Sharman

5. How many White Sox players were banned from baseball after the Black Sox Scandal of 1919?

    A. 6
    B. 7

C. 8
D. 9

6. 1920 was the first year of the Negro National League. Which team won the first pennant?

    A. Kansas City Monarchs
    B. Chicago American Giants
    C. Detroit Stars
    D. Indianapolis ABCs

7. During the 1921 season, Babe Ruth took the top spot for all-time home runs hit. What was the previous record, held by Roger Connor?

    A. 120
    B. 138
    C. 194
    D. 216

8. Which MLB rookie became the first player to notch five RBIs in his debut game?

    A. Wally Pipp
    B. Jack Fournier
    C. Gabby Hartnett
    D. Walter Mueller

9. Ty Cobb became the all-time leader in runs scored during the 1923 season. When he retired five years later, how many records did he hold?

    A. 14
    B. 67
    C. 90
    D. 114

10. In the first Colored World Series, the Kansas City Monarchs were victorious over which team?

    A. Philadelphia Hilldale Giants
    B. Baltimore Black Sox
    C. New York Lincoln Giants
    D. Harrisburg Giants

11. Lou Gehrig's ironman streak began in June of 1925. How did it begin?

    A. Started at first base
    B. Pinch hit
    C. Pinch run
    D. Relief pitcher

12. The Brooklyn Dodgers had tragedy strike twice when their owner, Charles Ebbetts, passed from a heart attack, and then his replacement, Edward McKeever, passed away how many days later?

    A. Seven
    B. Eight
    C. Nine
    D. Ten

13. During Game 4 of the 1926 World Series, Babe Ruth hit a home run that is still considered to be the longest in the history of the Series. How far did he hit it?

    A. 435 feet
    B. 466 feet
    C. 498 feet
    D. 530 feet

14. Which MLB team, with hitters nicknamed Murderers' Row, won the 1927 World Series?

    A. Philadelphia Athletics
    B. Pittsburgh Pirates
    C. New York Yankees
    D. New York Giants

15. True or False: Jesse and Virgil Barnes were the first brothers to pitch against each other in the MLB.

16. True or False: The 1928 Yankees were the first to sweep back-to-back World Series.

17. Which MLB team became the first to continuously use numbers on the backs of their jerseys, beginning with the 1929 season?

    A. Chicago Cubs
    B. Washington Senators

C. Brooklyn Robins
D. New York Yankees

18. The Philadelphia Phillies and St. Louis Cardinals set an MLB record for combined hits in a doubleheader. How many did they hit?

   A. 61
   B. 73
   C. 78
   D. 82

CHAPTER 5 ANSWERS:

1. B. ERA. Ruth posted an ERA of 1.75 that season.
2. C. 30. The Tigers won the game, 16-2.
3. D. 88. It did not help that the Black Sox Scandal during the 1919 World Series practically dismantled the team.
4. A. Eddie Grant. Though Grant was first, all the players listed as choices in this question were lost to the war.
5. C. Eight. Though no one was convicted of a crime, those eight were banned for fixing the Series or knowing about it.
6. B. Chicago American Giants. The team was managed by the founder of the league, Rube Foster.
7. B. 138. Ruth hit 59 home runs in that season alone.
8. D. Walter Mueller. The first pitch he ever faced also resulted in a home run for Mueller.
9. C. 90. He still holds several records, including career batting average, at .366.
10. A. Philadelphia Hilldale Giants. The Series went ten games, with Kansas City winning 5-4-1.
11. B. Pinch hit. It was the beginning of a legendary career.
12. B. Eight. McKeever passed after a bout of influenza.
13. D. 530 feet. It was his third home run of the game.
14. C. New York Yankees. They won the AL pennant that year by 19 games.
15. True. Virgil and the New York Giants defeated Jesse and the Brooklyn Robins.
16. True. They defeated the Pittsburgh Pirates in 1927 and the St. Louis Cardinals in 1928.
17. D. New York Yankees. The Cleveland Indians made a similar announcement just weeks later.
18. C. 73. The Cardinals lost the first game, 10-6, then won the second game, 28-6.

DID YOU KNOW?

Babe Ruth hit his 500th career home run during the 1929 season.

CHAPTER 6:
THE 1930S

1. Bill Terry became the first National League player to accomplish which feat?

    A. Bat over .400 in a season
    B. Hit 55 home runs
    C. Steal 50 bases
    D. Notch 150 strikeouts

2. True or False: The Sporting News selected the best player for each League in 1930 as there was no MVP award.

3. The 1931 season was the first for the Baseball Writers' Association of America to choose MVP award recipients. Who did they select from the AL in 1931?

    A. Frankie Frisch
    B. Lefty Grove
    C. Lou Gehrig
    D. Babe Ruth

4. Lou Gehrig's record number of RBIs in 1931 is unmatched in the American League to this day. How many did he hit?

    A. 166
    B. 179
    C. 185
    D. 197

5. True or False: Johnny Burnett went 9-for-11 in a July 10, 1932, game against the Athletics.

6. Babe Ruth famously called his shot during which game of the 1932 World Series?

    A. Game 1
    B. Game 2

C. Game 3
D. Game 4

7. The 1933 season marked the first All-Star Game. Where was it hosted?

   A. Detroit, Michigan
   B. New York, New York
   C. Philadelphia, Pennsylvania
   D. Chicago, Illinois

8. Babe Ruth made his final appearance on the mound during an October 1 game in 1933 against which team?

   A. Detroit Tigers
   B. Boston Red Sox
   C. New York Giants
   D. Chicago Cubs

9. True or False: In 1934, Shoeless Joe Jackson was reinstated to the MLB after his suspension from the 1919 World Series.

10. The Gashouse Gang defeated the Detroit Tigers in seven games to win the 1934 World Series. To which team did this nickname refer?

    A. St. Louis Cardinals
    B. New York Giants
    C. Chicago Cubs
    D. Boston Braves

11. On May 30, 1935, Babe Ruth retired from Major League Baseball, playing his final game with which team?

    A. New York Yankees
    B. Boston Red Sox
    C. Boston Braves
    D. Detroit Tigers

12. True or False: The Detroit Tigers won the World Series for the first time in 1935.

13. Which of these players was not part of the inaugural class of the National Baseball Hall of Fame, which debuted in 1936?

    A. Walter Johnson
    B. Christy Mathewson

- C. Honus Wagner
- D. Cy Young

14. Rookie Joe DiMaggio debuted on May 3, 1936, playing which position for the Yankees?
    - A. Right field
    - B. Left field
    - C. Center field
    - D. First base

15. Lefty Gomez won the AL Triple Crown in 1937, but Carl Hubbell of the NL led him in which category?
    - A. Wins
    - B. ERA
    - C. Strikeouts
    - D. Errors

16. True or False: Augie Galan became the first player to hit a home run from both sides of the plate in the same game.

17. True or False: In an August 2, 1938, game, the Dodgers and Cardinals experimented with an orange baseball for the first game of a doubleheader.

18. The Reds and Dodgers were the first teams to do what, on August 26, 1939?
    - A. Play a game in Mexico
    - B. Play a game in Europe
    - C. Play a game broadcast on television
    - D. Play a game that lasted 14 innings

CHAPTER 6 ANSWERS:

1. A. Bat over .400 in a season. His average even reached .406 at one point during the season.
2. True. They selected Joe Cronin of the Washington Senators and Bill Terry of the New York Giants.
3. B. Lefty Grove. Grove led in all the pitching categories for the year.
4. C. 185. He also tied Ruth with 46 home runs that year.
5. True. It is a record for the most hits in a game, and his team lost that game.
6. C. Game 3. Both Ruth and Gehrig hit two home runs that game.
7. D. Chicago, Illinois. The AL won the game, 4-2.
8. B. Boston Red Sox. The Yankees would win, 6-5.
9. False. He applied for reinstatement, but it was denied.
10. A. St. Louis Cardinals. They beat the Tigers 11-0 in Game 7 to win the Series.
11. C. Boston Braves. His last multi-home run game was on May 25 against Pittsburgh.
12. True. They lost their first four trips to the Series.
13. D. Cy Young. He was inducted one year later.
14. B. Left field. DiMaggio went 3-for-6 in his first game.
15. A. Wins. Hubbell had 22 to Gomez's 21.
16. True. He accomplished the feat on June 25, 1937.
17. False. They used a yellow ball!
18. C. Play a game broadcast on television. Red Barber served as the announcer.

DID YOU KNOW?

Joe DiMaggio batted .381 in 1939, earning MVP honors during his third season in the league.

CHAPTER 7:
THE 1940S

19. Bill McKechnie was the first manager to win the World Series with two different teams, the Pirates and which squad, that won it in 1940?

    A. Detroit Tigers
    B. Brooklyn Dodgers
    C. Cincinnati Reds
    D. St. Louis Browns

20. Which MLB team was the first to put a music organ into their stadium, in 1941?

    A. Chicago Cubs
    B. New York Yankees
    C. Brooklyn Dodgers
    D. St. Louis Cardinals

21. Ted Williams, in 1941, was the last player to ever do what?

    A. Hit for two cycles in two games
    B. Bat over .400 for a season
    C. Interrupt his career for military service
    D. Lead the AL in RBIs

22. Despite the attack on Pearl Harbor and the US entry into World War II, who wrote the "Green Light Letter" to encourage the MLB to keep playing?

    A. Dwight D. Eisenhower
    B. Harry S Truman
    C. Herbert Hoover
    D. Franklin Delano Roosevelt

23. Ted Williams enlisted into which branch of the US Military in June 1942?

    A. Army

B. Navy
  C. Air Force
  D. Marines

24. Which Yankees Pitcher was one category from a Pitching Triple Crown in 1943?

    A. Dizzy Trout
    B. Allie Reynolds
    C. Spud Chandler
    D. Elmer Riddle

25. True or False: The first night game played at Wrigley Field was the Girls League All-Star Game in 1943.

26. True or False: The 1944 World Series was called the "Street Buggy Series" as it featured both St. Louis teams.

27. How long did Joe Nuxhall, the youngest player to ever play in the MLB, last on the mound in his debut?

    A. 2 innings
    B. 1 inning
    C. 1/3 inning
    D. 2/3 inning

28. On September 8, 1945, Harry Truman threw a ceremonial pitch, setting two records. One is that he was the oldest president to throw one, but what was the other precedent?

    A. First left-handed president
    B. First underhand pitch from a president
    C. First pitch after a world war
    D. Biggest crowd for a presidential pitch

29. True or False: The curse of the Billy Goat began in October of 1945, fating the Cubs to decades of losing.

30. Danny Gardella, in February 1946, left the MLB in favor of which "outlaw" league?

    A. Canadian League
    B. Mexican League
    C. Japanese League
    D. Venezuelan League

31. For the first time in league history, what did every game on August 9, 1946, have in common?

    A. They were all morning games
    B. They were all doubleheaders
    C. They were all night games
    D. They all featured walk-off scores

32. True or False: Both the 1947 MLB World Series and All-American Girls Professional Baseball League championships were played between teams of the same state.

33. The first College World Series was won by which university?

    A. Michigan
    B. Florida
    C. Indiana
    D. California

34. Babe Ruth passed away on August 16, 1948, at what age?

    A. 65
    B. 53
    C. 69
    D. 77

35. Stan Musial led the NL in how many batting categories during the 1948 season?

    A. Five
    B. Six
    C. Seven
    D. Eight

36. True or False: Joe DiMaggio signed the first six-figure contract in the history of the sport in February 1949.

CHAPTER 7 ANSWERS:

1. C. Cincinnati Reds. They defeated the Tigers in seven games.
2. A. Chicago Cubs. Conversely, they waited 47 more years to install lights.
3. B. Bat over .400 for a season. He finished the 1941 season at .406.
4. D. Franklin Delano Roosevelt. The letter was sent to Commissioner Kenesaw Mountain Landis.
5. B. Navy. Williams would still win the Triple Crown for that season.
6. C. Spud Chandler. He was voted AL MVP that season, though.
7. True. They used temporary lights to play the game.
8. False. The Series was called the "Streetcar Series" and was won by the Cardinals.
9. D. 2/3 inning. His reliever, Jake Eisenhart, finished that inning but never played another MLB game.
10. A. First left-handed president. Washington beat St. Louis that day, 4-1.
11. True. William Sanis was kicked out of Game 4 of the World Series because of his goat, and the rest is history.
12. B. Mexican League. He would try to return a few years later, sparking a court battle.
13. C. They were all night games. Improving technology allowed more lighting at stadiums.
14. True. Both MLB teams were from New York, and both Girls teams were from Michigan.
15. D. California. They defeated Yale in the World Series.
16. B. 53. He passed due to cancer.
17. C. Seven. Batting average, runs, RBI, hits, doubles, triples, and slugging percentage.
18. True. It was a $100,000 contract with the Yankees.

DID YOU KNOW?

The New York Yankees retired Babe Ruth's number just nine weeks before Ruth passed away.

CHAPTER 8:
THE 1950S

1. Despite not leading any batting categories, which Yankees shortstop was voted AL MVP in 1950?

   A. Phil Rizzuto
   B. Billy Goodman
   C. Al Rosen
   D. Ralph Kiner

2. Vin Scully, legendary broadcaster, began his career on April 18, 1950, when he called how many innings of a 9-1 loss for the Brooklyn Dodgers?

   A. One
   B. Two
   C. Three
   D. Four

3. The "Shot Heard 'Round the World" helped determine which contest in 1951?

   A. The All-Star Game
   B. The AL Pennant
   C. The NL Pennant
   D. The World Series

4. Which New York Giants outfielder won a Rookie of the Year award in 1951?

   A. Gus Zernial
   B. Bobby Thomson
   C. Gil McDougald
   D. Willie Mays

5. True or False: In July 1952, Walt Dropo of the Tigers tied a league record with 12 consecutive hits in consecutive at-bats?

6. With the Yankees' 1952 World Series, they had won four in a row, and five of six. How many of those five titles came at the expense of the Brooklyn Dodgers?

   A. One
   B. Two
   C. Three
   D. Four

7. Which Cleveland Indian was the unanimous AL MVP in 1953?

   A. Dale Mitchell
   B. Bobby Avila
   C. Al Rosen
   D. Larry Doby

8. True or False: Billy Martin of the Yankees set the World Series record with 12 hits in the 1953 World Series.

9. Bobby Thomson broke his ankle sliding into a base during spring training of 1954. Who replaced him on the roster?

   A. Hank Aaron
   B. Jackie Robinson
   C. Wally Moon
   D. Bob Lemon

10. June Peppas pitched in the final game of the All-American Girls Professional Baseball League in 1954. What did she accomplish?

    A. Perfect game
    B. No-hitter
    C. Complete game
    D. 20 strikeouts

11. True or False: The Dodgers finally topped the Yankees in the 1955 World Series after several defeats.

12. Beginning with the 1955 season, the MLB created a new rule to speed up the game. It stated that pitchers must deliver the ball within how many seconds of taking a pitching position?

    A. 15 seconds
    B. 20 seconds
    C. 30 seconds
    D. 40 seconds

13. Who won the first-ever Cy Young Award for the best pitching performance of 1956?

    A. Lew Burdette
    B. Sam Jones
    C. Don Newcombe
    D. Whitey Ford

14. True or False: Mickey Mantle won the batting Triple Crown in the American League during the 1956 season.

15. The first MLB game played on the west coast of the United States was won by which team?

    A. St. Louis Cardinals
    B. Cincinnati Reds
    C. Los Angeles Dodgers
    D. San Francisco Giants

16. True or False: The 1958 Yankees became the third team to come back from a 3-1 deficit to win the World Series.

17. Don Drysdale is the only pitcher in league history to do what on two opening-day games in a row?

    A. Hit a home run
    B. Throw a no-hitter
    C. Throw a shutout
    D. Throw a complete game

18. True or False: The Dodgers defeated the White Sox in six games to win the 1959 World Series.

CHAPTER 8 ANSWERS:

1. A. Phil Rizzuto. It helped that the Yankees won another pennant and another World Series.
2. B. Two. Scully's career would last for 66 years, a record in baseball broadcasting.
3. C. The NL Pennant. The Giants defeated the Dodgers.
4. D. Willie Mays. His team would lose in the World Series to the Yankees, though.
5. True. It is a record shared with two other players.
6. C. Three. It was a lopsided rivalry.
7. C. Al Rosen. He hit 43 home runs and 145 RBIs that season.
8. True. It was yet another victory for the Yankees over the Dodgers.
9. A. Hank Aaron. It was the start of a great career.
10. C. Complete game. The Kalamazoo Lassies won the game, 8-5.
11. True. They won the Series in seven games.
12. B. 20 seconds. Speeding up the game has been an issue for decades.
13. C. Don Newcombe. He also won the NL MVP award that season.
14. True. Mantle hit 52 homers and 130 RBIs that season.
15. D. San Francisco Giants. They shut out the Los Angeles Dodgers on April 15, 1958.
16. False. At the time, the Yankees were only the second team to achieve the feat.
17. A. Hit a home run. The Dodgers still lost the game, though.
18. True. It was the team's second title, and their first while in Los Angeles.

DID YOU KNOW?

The 1959 World Series was the first in which neither team had a pitcher pitch a complete game.

CHAPTER 9:

THE 1960S

1. True or False: Ted Williams became the first MLB player to hit a home run in four different decades.

2. What solution did Baltimore manager Paul Richards devise to help the team's passed-ball problem in 1960?

    A. He had his catchers stay on their knees
    B. He stopped allowing knuckleballs
    C. He created a bigger catcher's mitt
    D. He instructed his pitchers to keep pitches higher

3. The Los Angeles Angels played their first game on April 11, 1961. Who did they play?

    A. Baltimore Orioles
    B. Kansas City Athletics
    C. Washington Senators
    D. Minnesota Twins

4. In a doubleheader on September 14, 1961, the Cardinals and Cubs set a league record by using how many players?

    A. 64
    B. 68
    C. 72
    D. 75

5. True or False: Tommy John was a pitcher signed by the Cleveland Indians in 1961.

6. Gil Hodges and Charlie Neal hit home runs for which new team in their first game, on April 11, 1962?

    A. Houston Colt .45s
    B. New York Mets
    C. Kansas City Athletics
    D. Washington Senators

7. Which 1963 Cy Young, MVP, and World Series MVP award winner played for the LA Dodgers?

   A. Gary Peters
   B. Juan Marichal
   C. Whitey Ford
   D. Sandy Koufax

8. The Yankees released which player at the end of the 1963 season, then immediately brought him back as their manager?

   A. Mickey Mantle
   B. Yogi Berra
   C. Whitey Ford
   D. Roger Maris

9. Jim Bunning notched ten strikeouts on June 21, 1964, on his way to a perfect game against which team?

   A. New York Mets
   B. Philadelphia Phillies
   C. Chicago White Sox
   D. Pittsburgh Pirates

10. The fifth-place Cardinals replaced their manager with 45 games left in the 1964 season. What was the result with Bob Howsam on the bench?

    A. Third place
    B. Second place
    C. Reached World Series
    D. Won World Series

11. Sandy Koufax dominated during the 1965 season, earning the pitching Triple Crown. How many strikeouts did he register that year?

    A. 289
    B. 334
    C. 382
    D. 419

12. True or False: The Kansas City Athletics' Satchel Paige became the oldest pitcher to play in the MLB at age 54, when he played on September 25, 1965.

13. True or False: Sandy Koufax won another pitching Triple Crown in 1966, with an even lower ERA than his previous season.

14. The New York Mets won the rights to Tom Seaver after which team improperly signed him to a minor league contract while he was still in college?

    A. Cleveland Indians
    B. Atlanta Braves
    C. Philadelphia Phillies
    D. Washington Senators

15. Which player won the 1967 AL Triple Crown in batting, but his team fell short in the World Series?

    A. Roberto Clemente
    B. Hank Aaron
    C. Harmon Killebrew
    D. Carl Yastrzemski

16. True or False: Four teams finished within three games of the AL pennant to end the 1967 season.

17. The 1968 season featured which low batting average that was good enough for the AL batting title?

    A. .296
    B. .301
    C. .311
    D. .315

18. Of the four expansion teams that joined in 1969, which one finished with the best record?

    A. San Diego Padres
    B. Kansas City Royals
    C. Seattle Pilots
    D. Montreal Expos

CHAPTER 9 ANSWERS:

1. True. He accomplished the feat on Opening Day of the 1960 season.
2. C. He created a bigger catcher's mitt. It was 50% larger and 40 ounces heavier.
3. A. Baltimore Orioles. The Angels won 7-2.
4. C. 72. The Cardinals won both games.
5. True. Though, he is mostly known today for the injury and surgery named after him.
6. B. New York Mets. They lost their first game, 11-4.
7. D. Sandy Koufax. He also won the pitching Triple Crown in 1963.
8. B. Yogi Berra. He managed the team for one season, then returned to the field a year later, but with the Mets.
9. A. New York Mets. It was the first perfect game since 1922.
10. D. Won World Series. The team went 31-14 under the new manager.
11. C. 382. Koufax won 26 games with a 2.04 ERA that year.
12. False. His approximate age was 59. He got one strikeout and gave up one hit in the appearance.
13. True. He posted a 1.73 ERA in 1966, down from 2.04.
14. B. Atlanta Braves. It is one of those tiny details that changes a big chunk of baseball history.
15. D. Carl Yastrzemski. He hit 44 home runs and 121 RBIs.
16. True. The Tigers and Twins both finished one game back of the Red Sox.
17. B. .301. It remains the lowest mark for either league's batting champion.
18. B. Kansas City Royals. They finished with 69 wins. Seattle had 64, the other two had 52.

DID YOU KNOW?

The 1969 season was the first to feature an expanded playoff format.

CHAPTER 10:
THE 1970S

1. Which pitcher became the first to pitch in 1,000 MLB games?

    A. Wayne Granger
    B. Hoyt Wilhelm
    C. Bert Blyleven
    D. Steve Hamilton

2. Dock Ellis of the Pittsburgh Pirates claimed that he threw a no-hitter on June 12 of 1970 while under the influence of what drug?

    A. LSD
    B. Marijuana
    C. Heroin
    D. Alcohol

3. Joe Torre of the St. Louis Cardinals missed out on the 1971 Triple Crown for batting by which lone category?

    A. Batting average
    B. RBIs
    C. Home Runs
    D. Walks

4. The longest shutout in AL history happened on July 9, 1971, between the Athletics and Angels. How many innings did the 1-0 game last?

    A. 17
    B. 18
    C. 19
    D. 20

5. True or False: Sandy Koufax was inducted into the Hall of Fame at age 36, the youngest to earn the honor.

6. True or False: The American League, in 1972, voted to adopt the designated hitter rule for a three-year experimental basis.

7. All-Star Roberto Clemente died in a plane crash on his way to which country?

   A. Nicaragua
   B. Costa Rica
   C. Colombia
   D. Mexico

8. Reggie Jackson had a career year in 1973, but which of these did he not accomplish?

   A. Lead the AL in home runs
   B. Win World Series MVP
   C. Lead the AL in batting average
   D. Lead the AL in RBIs

9. Which MLB team experimented with orange baseballs during an exhibition game in March 1973?

   A. Cleveland Indians
   B. Oakland Athletics
   C. Atlanta Braves
   D. New York Yankees

10. The Cleveland Indians caused themselves a lot of trouble when they ran this promotion for a home game in June 1974.

    A. Bobblehead day
    B. Free popcorn
    C. Free hot dogs
    D. Ten-cent beers

11. True or False: Frank Robinson became the first Black manager when he was hired in 1974 to take over the Atlanta Braves.

12. True or False: Tom Seaver missed out on the pitching Triple Crown in the ERA category after the 1975 season.

13. The Cincinnati Reds came from behind in how many of their victories during the 1975 World Series?

    A. Four
    B. Three
    C. Two
    D. One

14. Carl Yastrzemski got his 2500th hit on July 26, 1976, but who accomplished the feat one week prior?

    A. Ernie Banks
    B. Rod Carew
    C. Willie Davis
    D. Al Kaline

15. George Brett edged which teammate of his to win the 1976 AL batting title?

    A. Ken Griffey
    B. Hal McRae
    C. Bill Madlock
    D. Tony Taylor

16. What was the result of the Seattle Mariners' first-ever game?

    A. 7-0 loss to Kansas City Royals
    B. 7-0 loss to San Francisco Giants
    C. 7-0 loss to San Diego Padres
    D. 7-0 loss to California Angels

17. Why did an umpire crew walk off in protest during an April 17, 1977, game in Atlanta?

    A. Fans were heckling them
    B. The video screen showed a controversial replay
    C. The players refused to leave after ejections
    D. They thought the nearby storm was too close

18. True or False: Joe and Phil Niekro tied for the most NL pitching wins during the 1979 season.

CHAPTER 10 ANSWERS:

1. B. Hoyt Wilhelm. His nickname was "Old Sarge".
2. A. LSD. That no-hitter was against the San Diego Padres.
3. C. Home Runs. Willie Stargell hit 48 that season.
4. D. 20. Both teams combined for 43 strikeouts, another record.
5. True. He was inducted on January 19, 1972.
6. True. They would vote to keep the change permanent in 1975.
7. A. Nicaragua. He was helping bring charity and aid to victims of an earthquake at the time.
8. C. Lead the AL in batting average. Jackson also won AL MVP that year.
9. B. Oakland Athletics. The team lost that game, 11-5, and the idea did not stick.
10. D. Ten-cent beers. The drunken mayhem spread from the stands and down onto the field. Cleveland had to forfeit after fans rushed the field in the ninth inning.
11. False. Robinson was hired by the Cleveland Indians.
12. True. Randy Jones from San Diego led the NL in ERA that season, with a 2.25.
13. A. Four. Each game was a comeback victory, helped by MVP Pete Rose.
14. C. Willie Davis. He accomplished the feat against the Cubs on July 19, 1976.
15. B. Hal McRae. McRae accused Steve Brye of racism, as Brett's clinching hit bounced over Brye's head in the outfield.
16. D. 7-0 loss to California Angels. It was also the first MLB game played in the Kingdome.
17. B. The video screen showed a controversial replay. The umps returned when they were assured it would not happen again.
18. True. They both notched 21 wins that season.

DID YOU KNOW?

Pete Rose is the only player in MLB history to play five different positions at MLB All-Star Games.

CHAPTER 11:
THE 1980S

1. How long was Al Cowens suspended by the AL for attacking White Sox pitcher Ed Farmer on June 20, 1980?
   A. 60 games
   B. Two months
   C. One week
   D. Ten days

2. The Kansas City Royals win the AL pennant after defeating which team in the 1980 ALCS?
   A. New York Yankees
   B. Detroit Tigers
   C. Baltimore Orioles
   D. Boston Red Sox

3. What caused the MLB to expand the number of playoff teams temporarily in 1981?
   A. Proposal from owners
   B. More teams added to league
   C. Player strike
   D. Experiment from commissioner

4. The longest professional baseball game in history took place on June 23, 1981. How long did it last?
   A. 31 innings
   B. 32 innings
   C. 33 innings
   D. 34 innings

5. True or False: Hank Aaron's Hall of Fame election percentage is second only to Ty Cobb.

6. Which MLB player made his debut on May 30, 1982, his first game of 2,632 in a row?

A. Bob Boone
   B. Cal Ripkin Jr.
   C. Joel Youngblood
   D. Dave Stapleton

7. Which MLB pitcher was the first to 300 saves, achieved on August 8, 1982?

   A. Gaylord Perry
   B. Roger Clemens
   C. Nolan Ryan
   D. Rollie Fingers

8. True or False: Nolan Ryan took over the top spot on the career strikeout list with his 4,197th K in April 1983.

9. In July 1983, George Brett had a home run taken away, then restored after protest, in a game now known as what?

   A. The Corked Bat Game
   B. The Pine Tar Game
   C. The Stolen Homer Game
   D. The Spitball Game

10. The 1984 Detroit Tigers were the fourth MLB team in history to hold first place for the entire season. Which of these teams did not accomplish that feat?

    A. 1923 New York Giants
    B. 1927 New York Yankees
    C. 1955 Brooklyn Dodgers
    D. 1971 New York Yankees

11. Reggie Jackson was the first player to hit 100 home runs with three different teams. Which of these was not one of those teams?

    A. California Angels
    B. Oakland Athletics
    C. Baltimore Orioles
    D. New York Yankees

12. True or False: The Braves still shot off July 4 fireworks despite the night's game lasting until 3 a.m. on July 5, 1985.

13. Roger Clemens led the AL in wins and ERA during the 1986 season. How many wins did he notch?

A. 23
B. 24
C. 25
D. 26

14. On July 29, 1986, Sparky Anderson became the first manager to win how many games in both the AL and NL?

    A. 600
    B. 700
    C. 750
    D. 800

15. The Minnesota Twins won the 1987 World Series over which team?

    A. San Francisco Giants
    B. New York Mets
    C. Cincinnati Reds
    D. St. Louis Cardinals

16. Jose Canseco led the AL in home runs during the 1988 season. Who led the NL?

    A. Tony Gwynn
    B. Will Clark
    C. Darryl Strawberry
    D. Wade Boggs

17. True or False: On September 20, 1988, Wade Boggs became the first player since 1901 to get 200 hits in six straight seasons.

18. True or False: Kirk Gibson's home run in Game 1 of the 1988 World Series is the inspiration for the phrase "walk-off home run."

CHAPTER 11 ANSWERS:

1. C. One week. Cowens had been hit by a Farmer pitch the year before. It broke Cowens' jaw and caused him to miss 21 games.
2. A. New York Yankees. The Royals had lost to the Yankees in the ALCS in 1976, 1977, and 1978.
3. C. Player strike. The winner of each division from each half of the season made the playoffs.
4. C. 33 innings. The Pawtucket Red Sox defeated the Rochester Red Wings, 3-2.
5. True. Aaron was nine votes shy of being the first unanimous selection.
6. B. Cal Ripkin Jr. The ironman streak had begun.
7. D. Rollie Fingers. He helped the Brewers beat the Mariners that day.
8. False. He did get to the top of the list, but it was only his 3,509th strikeout at the time.
9. B. The Pine Tar Game. The game was finished almost a month later, on August 18.
10. D. 1971 New York Yankees. The Tigers would go on to win the World Series.
11. C. Baltimore Orioles. Jackson only played one season there.
12. True. The Braves lost 16-13 in 19 innings.
13. B. 24. His ERA was 2.48, leading the Sox to the AL Pennant.
14. A. 600. His wins came with Detroit and Cincinnati.
15. D. St. Louis Cardinals. The Series went the full seven games.
16. C. Darryl Strawberry. He hit 39 homers with the Mets in 1988.
17. True. Boggs also became the second player to get 200 hits and 100 bases on balls in three straight years.
18. True. His iconic moment at the plate spurred his team to victory.

DID YOU KNOW?

The SkyDome in Toronto was the first stadium with a working retractable roof.

CHAPTER 12:
THE 1990S

1. How long did the 32-day lockout in 1990 delay the beginning of the season?

    A. One week
    B. Ten days
    C. Two weeks
    D. Three weeks

2. Who was the first player to win a batting title in three different decades?

    A. Wade Boggs
    B. Hank Aaron
    C. George Brett
    D. Willie McGee

3. Jose Canseco and Cecil Fielder each hit how many home runs during the 1991 season?

    A. 44
    B. 45
    C. 46
    D. 47

4. During the 1991 season, a record number of managers were fired across the league. How many?

    A. 12
    B. 13
    C. 14
    D. 15

5. True or False: Pete Rose received 41 write-in votes for the Hall of Fame in 1992 despite his lifetime ban.

6. In November of 1992, an expansion draft is held for two new franchises, the Florida Marlins and which team?

A. Washington Nationals
   B. Houston Astros
   C. Arizona Diamondbacks
   D. Colorado Rockies

7. Tim Crews and Steve Olin passed away in a boating accident in March 1993. Which team did they play for?

   A. Detroit Tigers
   B. Oakland Athletics
   C. Cleveland Indians
   D. New York Yankees

8. Fred McGriff, just traded to Atlanta, was able to play a July 20, 1993, game thanks to a delay from what?

   A. Protests outside stadium
   B. Fire in the press box
   C. Power outage
   D. Thunderstorm

9. Basketball legend Michael Jordan suited up for the Birmingham Barons in 1994, which was an affiliate of which MLB team?

   A. Chicago White Sox
   B. Detroit Tigers
   C. Atlanta Braves
   D. Cincinnati Reds

10. True or False: The remainder of the 1994 season was canceled on September 14 because of a players' strike.

11. True or False: The 1995 season was the first to expand the playoffs, and the first to include Wild Card entries.

12. Which Atlanta Braves pitcher was named the MVP of the 1995 World Series?

    A. Greg Maddux
    B. Tom Glavine
    C. John Smoltz
    D. Steve Avery

13. Which slugger led the NL in home runs and RBIs during the 1996 season?

A. Mark McGwire
B. Tony Gwynn
C. Andres Galarraga
D. Alex Rodriguez

14. Barry Bonds became the second member of which exclusive MLB club during the 1996 season?

    A. 50-home run club
    B. 150-RBI club
    C. 40-40 club
    D. 500-home run club

15. The Florida Marlins shocked the baseball world by winning the World Series despite what?

    A. Coming from behind in each series
    B. Being a wild card team
    C. Falling behind to the Yankees
    D. Being in their second year of existence

16. True or False: In 1997, Sandy Alomar Jr. was the first hometown player to hit a home run at the All-Star Game since Joe DiMaggio did it in 1972.

17. Which of these four players won the home run race of 1998?

    A. Sammy Sosa
    B. Ken Griffey Jr.
    C. Mark McGwire
    D. Greg Vaughn

18. True or False: The Tampa Bay Devil Rays won their first franchise game over the Detroit Tigers, 11-8.

CHAPTER 12 ANSWERS:

1. A. One week. It also eliminated spring training for that year.
2. C. George Brett. He won in 1976, 1980, and 1990.
3. A. 44. Fielder led in RBIs, with 133.
4. B. 13. The last firing of the year happened when Jim Essian was fired by the Cubs on October 18, 1991.
5. True. Rose was banned for gambling on games.
6. D. Colorado Rockies. 72 players are chosen in the draft.
7. C. Cleveland Indians. A third player, Bob Ojeda, was injured in the crash.
8. B. Fire in the press box. He hit a game-tying two-run home run in the sixth, helping the team rally to victory.
9. A. Chicago White Sox. Jordan went 0-for-3 in his debut.
10. True. No World Series was played that year.
11. True. Both Wild Card teams lost their series that year.
12. B. Tom Glavine. Maddux led the NL in wins and ERA during the year, though.
13. C. Andres Galarraga. He hit 47 homers and 150 RBIs for the Rockies.
14. C. 40-40 club. He hit 40 homers and stole 40 bases in one season. Only four other players have done it in league history.
15. B. Being a wild card team. They swept San Francisco to start their great run.
16. False. Hank Aaron was the last player to accomplish the feat in 1972.
17. C. Mark McGwire. They all had reached 30 homers by the All-Star break: the first time four players accomplished it in the same year.
18. True. Fred McGriff contributed four RBIs in the victory.

DID YOU KNOW?

Pedro Martinez won the 1999 Triple Crown in pitching for the Boston Red Sox.

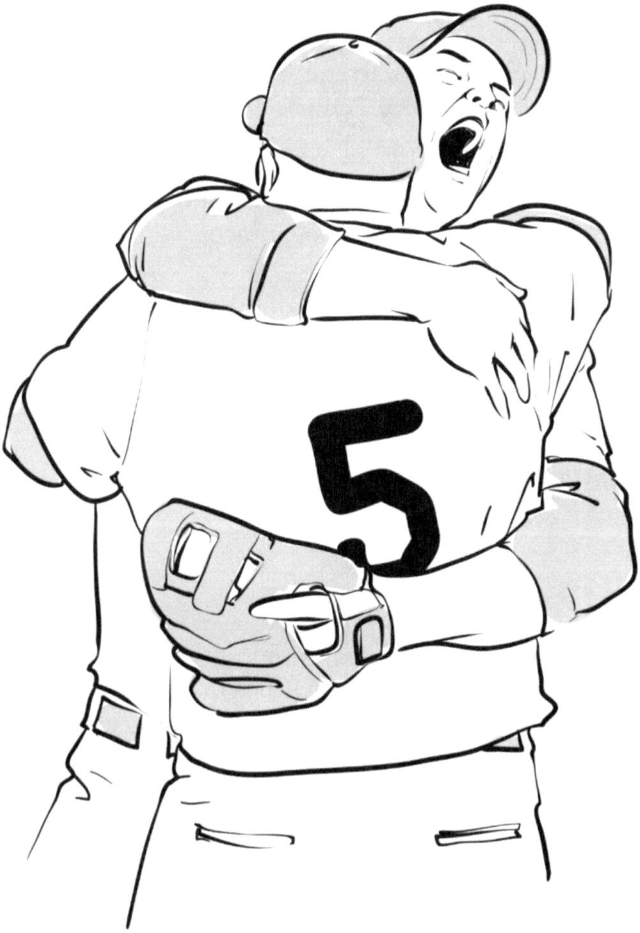
5

CHAPTER 13:

THE 2000S

1. True or False: Andres Galarraga hit a home run in his first game back from cancer surgery, which had caused him to miss the entire 1999 season.

2. Randy Johnson had an incredible month of April during the 2000 season. How many of his six appearances were complete games?
   A. Two
   B. Three
   C. Four
   D. Five

3. Ichiro Suzuki and Larry Walker won the batting titles for the AL and NL in 2001, both with what batting average?
   A. .340
   B. .350
   C. .360
   D. .361

4. The Cleveland Indians tied an MLB record when they came back from how many runs down against the Seattle Mariners on August 5, 2001?
   A. 10
   B. 11
   C. 12
   D. 13

5. The 2002 Diamondbacks became the first defending champions since 1919 to do what?
   A. Lose the opening game of the season in a shutout
   B. Win their first two regular season games in shutouts
   C. Completely change their pitching staff
   D. Fire their manager less than 20 games into the season

6. The 2002 Angels' John Lackey became the first rookie to win Game 7 of a World Series since what year?

   A. 1909
   B. 1917
   C. 1933
   D. 1954

7. The 2003 Detroit Tigers finished with the most losses in AL history. How many games did they lose?

   A. 116
   B. 117
   C. 118
   D. 119

8. True or False: In 2003, Alex Rodriguez became the youngest player to reach 300 home runs at 27 years and 249 days of age.

9. The Curse of the Bambino came to an end when which team won the 2004 World Series?

   A. Chicago Cubs
   B. Boston Red Sox
   C. Florida Marlins
   D. Minnesota Twins

10. Barry Bonds set the record for on-base percentage in 2004 with what rate?

    A. .582
    B. .590
    C. .609
    D. .615

11. True or False: The 2005 Chicago White Sox only lost one playoff game on their way to the World Series championship.

12. The longest-ever postseason game (at the time) took place between the Astros and Braves in the 2005 NLDS. How many innings did it take?

    A. 16
    B. 17
    C. 18
    D. 19

13. Which of these four teams won the 2006 World Baseball Classic?

    A. Japan
    B. Cuba
    C. Dominican Republic
    D. Korea

14. The 2006 Florida Marlins were the first team to have this many rookie pitchers get ten wins in the same season.

    A. Five
    B. Two
    C. Three
    D. Four

15. True or False: Five of the seven playoff series during the 2007 playoffs were sweeps.

16. During a game in 2008, Randy Johnson became the first pitcher to do what with two different teams?

    A. Throw 2,000 strikeouts
    B. Win 100 games
    C. Notch an ERA under 2
    D. Win 80 games

17. September 19, 2008, was the first time an instant replay was used to overturn a call, giving a home run to which team?

    A. Tampa Bay Rays
    B. Minnesota Twins
    C. Chicago Cubs
    D. Philadelphia Phillies

18. True or False: The 2009 Yankees set an MLB record by playing 18 straight games without committing an error.

CHAPTER 13 ANSWERS:

1. True. It was against his former team, the Colorado Rockies.
2. B. Three. He had two shutouts and an ERA of 0.91.
3. B. .350. Neither of them led in RBIs or home runs, though.
4. C. 12. They were down 14-2 but found a way back.
5. B. Win their first two regular season games in shutouts. Having Randy Johnson helped!
6. A. 1909. It was the first title for the Angels.
7. D. 119. They were one loss away from tying the MLB record from the 1962 Mets.
8. True. He passed Jimmie Foxx's record by almost 80 days.
9. B. Boston Red Sox. They had not won since 1918.
10. C. .609. He broke the previous record of .582, which he also owned.
11. True. They swept the Red Sox, defeated the Angels 4-1, then the Astros 4-0.
12. C. 18. It was also the first playoff game to have two grand slams.
13. A. Japan. Ichiro Suzuki and Daisuke Matsuzaka both helped in the victory.
14. D. Four. Anibal Sanchez was the fourth to reach the ten-win mark that year.
15. True. Only the ALDS between Cleveland and New York and ALCS were not sweeps.
16. A. Throw 2,000 strikeouts. He passed the mark with Arizona in a win over the Cubs.
17. A. Tampa Bay Rays. Carlos Pena benefited from the changed call.
18. True. The streak ended during game 19 when Jorge Posada made a throwing error.

DID YOU KNOW?

The 2009 season needed a tiebreaker, marking the third season in a row that the season went beyond 162 games. Three seasons is the longest streak of such an occurrence.

CHAPTER 14:

THE 2010S

1. True or False: Roy Halladay pitched a no-hitter against the Florida Marlins on May 29, 2010.

2. The National League won the 2010 All-Star Game, for the first time since 1996. Who was the MVP?

   A. Joey Votto
   B. Brian McCann
   C. Rafael Furcal
   D. Chase Utley

3. Manny Ramirez decided to retire at the beginning of the 2011 season, as he was facing a suspension of how many games?

   A. 50
   B. 60
   C. 80
   D. 100

4. The 2011 White Sox were swept at home for the first time since which year, in a series against the Yankees?

   A. 1945
   B. 1958
   C. 1976
   D. 1991

5. The MLB expanded its playoff format in 2012 to ten teams. Which Wild Card team survived the Divisional Round in 2012?

   A. St. Louis Cardinals
   B. Atlanta Braves
   C. Baltimore Orioles
   D. Texas Rangers

6. True or False: Justin Upton and B.J. Upton were the first brother pairing to reach 100 home runs each on the same day.

7. Which team ended its North American sports league record 20-year streak of losing seasons in 2013?

   A. Cincinnati Reds
   B. Pittsburgh Pirates
   C. New York Mets
   D. Toronto Blue Jays

8. Alex Rodriguez hit his 24th career grand slam on September 20, 2013, surpassing which legend?

   A. Babe Ruth
   B. Hank Aaron
   C. Lou Gehrig
   D. Willie Mays

9. Madison Bumgarner and Buster Posey are the only pitcher-catcher battery to achieve what feat, accomplished on July 13, 2014?

   A. Both hit game-tying triples
   B. Both hit for the cycle
   C. Both tally five RBIs
   D. Both hit grand slams

10. True or False: Derek Jeter holds the record for the most AL games played at shortstop.

11. On August 11, 2015, what did all 15 games have in common for the first time in league history?

    A. All the away teams won
    B. All the home teams won
    C. Each game required extra innings
    D. Each game ended with a score

12. Which MLB team was the first to hire a female coach, in September 2015?

    A. Detroit Tigers
    B. Oakland Athletics
    C. Chicago Cubs
    D. New York Yankees

13. True or False: The Cardinals were the first team to have three pinch hitters hit home runs in the same game.

14. After their pitcher, Jose Fernandez, died in a boating accident, which team canceled their game against the Atlanta Braves later that day, on September 25, 2016?

    A. Miami Marlins
    A. Los Angeles Dodgers
    B. Boston Red Sox
    C. Philadelphia Phillies

15. The Houston Astros won the 2017 World Series, ending a drought of how many years?

    A. 45
    B. 51
    C. 56
    D. 61

16. Mookie Betts won the 2018 AL MVP Award, but he was likely happier to win the 2018 World Series with which team?

    A. Boston Red Sox
    B. Los Angeles Dodgers
    C. Houston Astros
    D. Milwaukee Brewers

17. The Arizona Diamondbacks began using a bullpen car in 2018, the first time one was used in the league since which year?

    A. 1991
    B. 1988
    C. 1995
    D. 2000

18. True or False: Ronald Acuna Jr's $100 million, eight-year extension made him the youngest player to sign a deal for nine figures in the league's history.

CHAPTER 14 ANSWERS:

1. False. Halladay pitched a perfect game on that day, winning 1-0.
2. B. Brian McCann. He scored all three RBIs in a 3-1 victory.
3. D. 100. He had tested positive for banned substances for the second time.
4. C. 1976. Yankees' pitchers did not allow a base on balls during the four-game sweep.
5. A. St. Louis Cardinals. They defeated Atlanta, then Washington before losing to San Francisco in the NLCS.
6. True. They accomplished the feat on August 3, 2012.
7. B. Pittsburgh Pirates. They won their 81st game of the season on September 3, 2013.
8. C. Lou Gehrig. Rodriguez remains at the top of the career grand slam list.
9. D. Both hit grand slams. Bumgarner was the most recent pitcher to hit two grand slams in a season since 1966.
10. True. Omar Vizquel holds the MLB record, with 2,709 games, 35 more than Jeter.
11. B. All the home teams won. Home teams were 11-0 on September 16, 1989.
12. B. Oakland Athletics. They hired Dr. Justine Siegal for their 2015 Instructional League club.
13. True. They accomplished the feat on April 8, 2016.
14. A. Miami Marlins. Fernandez passed in a boating accident in Miami Beach.
15. C. 56. They defeated the Dodgers in seven games to win.
16. A. Boston Red Sox. They defeated the Dodgers four games to one.
17. C. 1995. It was first used in the MLB in 1950.
18. True. He is also the fastest to 25 homers, just 92 games.

DID YOU KNOW?

The 2013 season was the first since 1996 that the BBWAA election resulted in no selections to the Baseball Hall of Fame.

CHAPTER 15:
TEAMS COMING AND GOING

1. Which MLB team was born as the Milwaukee Brewers in 1901?
   A. Baltimore Orioles
   B. Atlanta Braves
   C. Milwaukee Brewers
   D. New York Yankees

2. The Indianapolis Hoosiers became which of these teams in 1914?
   A. Washington Senators
   B. Newark Peppers
   C. Louisville Colonels
   D. New York Yankees

3. The Washington Senators moved northwest to become which current MLB team in 1960?
   A. Cleveland Indians
   B. Detroit Tigers
   C. Minnesota Twins
   D. Milwaukee Brewers

4. The 1961-71 version of the Washington Senators became which team out west?
   A. San Francisco Giants
   B. Seattle Mariners
   C. California Angels
   D. Texas Rangers

5. For how many years did the Montreal Expos exist before moving to Washington?
   A. 31
   B. 36
   C. 41
   D. 44

6. The New York Giants existed how many years longer than the Brooklyn Dodgers before they both left for California in 1957?

   A. One
   B. Two
   C. Three
   D. Four

7. The Cleveland Spiders went defunct in which year when the National League contracted?

   A. 1895
   B. 1898
   C. 1899
   D. 1902

8. Which of these teams did not fold due to the disbanding of the Federal League in 1915?

   A. Brooklyn Tip-Tops
   B. Baltimore Terrapins
   C. Chicago Whales
   D. Louisville Colonels

9. Which of these teams disbanded after 1892?

   A. Columbus Solons
   B. Pittsburgh Stogies
   C. Cleveland Infants
   D. St. Louis Terriers

10. The Boston Braves would eventually end up in Atlanta, but where did they play in 1953–1965?

    A. Milwaukee
    B. Detroit
    C. Indianapolis
    D. St. Louis

11. The St. Louis Browns became which team in 1953?

    A. Atlanta Braves
    B. Cincinnati Reds
    C. Baltimore Orioles
    D. Washington Nationals

12. Which of these was not a real Negro League team?

A. Indianapolis ABCs
   B. Indianapolis Athletics
   C. Indianapolis Clowns
   D. Indianapolis Browns

13. Which of these defunct teams from the 1800s won at least one pennant in their existence?
    A. Detroit Wolverines
    B. New York Mutuals
    C. Hartford Dark Blues
    D. Louisville Grays

14. Of all the MLB teams to relocate or disband, which one lasted the longest prior to moving?
    A. New York Giants
    B. Boston Braves
    C. Brooklyn Dodgers
    D. Washington Senators

15. The Boston Braves would eventually end up in Atlanta, but where did they play from 1953–1965?
    A. Milwaukee
    B. Detroit
    C. Indianapolis
    D. St. Louis

16. The New York Giants began playing in 1883 under what team name, before switching two years later?
    A. Metropolitans
    B. Brown Stockings
    C. Gothams
    D. Knickerbockers

17. The 1901–1902 Baltimore Orioles disbanded, but their history can be connected to which current MLB team?
    A. New York Yankees
    B. New York Mets
    C. Philadelphia Phillies
    D. Pittsburgh Pirates

18. True or False: The New York Highlanders changed their name to the Yankees ten years after beginning play.

CHAPTER 15 ANSWERS:

1. A. Baltimore Orioles. The original Brewers only lasted one season, in 1901.
2. B. Newark Peppers. The Peppers were around for three years in the Federal League.
3. C. Minnesota Twins. The franchise has won three World Series between the two cities.
4. D. Texas Rangers. They won their first championship in 2023.
5. B. 36. They left Montreal in 2004.
6. A. One. The Dodgers formed in 1884; the Giants in 1883.
7. C. 1899. They had lasted 13 years before folding.
8. D. Louisville Colonels. They disbanded in 1899 with the Spiders!
9. D. St. Louis Terriers. They disbanded in 1915.
10. A. Milwaukee. The Milwaukee Braves lasted 13 years before the move to Atlanta.
11. C. Baltimore Orioles. The St. Louis Browns lasted 52 years before the move.
12. D. Indianapolis Browns. The Clowns played from 1943 to 1948.
13. A. Detroit Wolverines. They won one pennant and folded in 1888.
14. B. Boston Braves. They lasted 77 seasons, two more than the Giants.
15. A. Milwaukee. They won the World Series in 1957.
16. C. Gothams. After they switched names, they won championships only a few years later.
17. A. New York Yankees. They were established the next season.
18. True. The Highlanders became the Yankees in 1913.

DID YOU KNOW?

The Yankees hold the MLB record with 27 World Series championships.

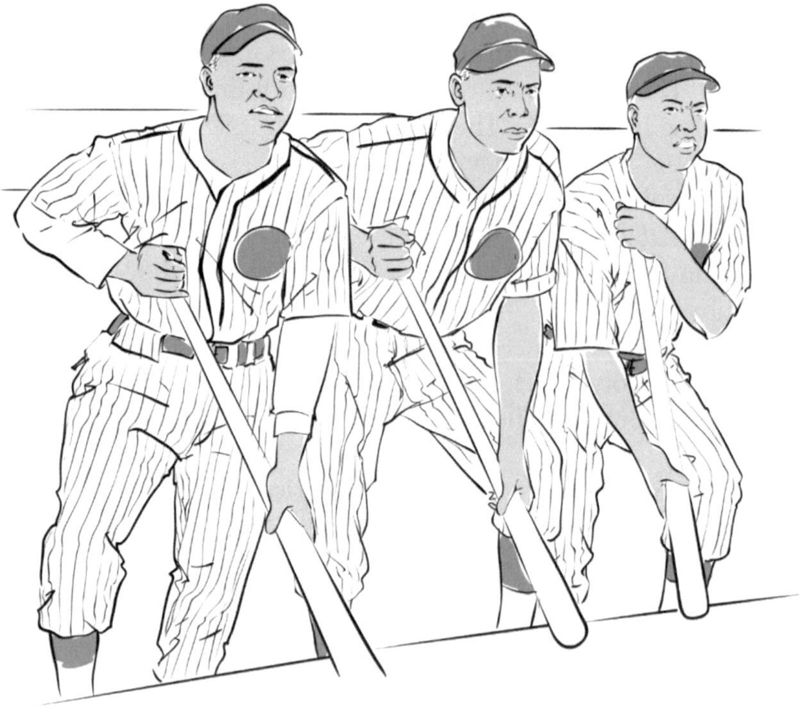

CHAPTER 16:
FORMER LEAGUES & DIVISIONS

1. Big League Baseball worked similarly to Little League, but only allowed which age bracket?

    A. 13-15
    B. 14-16
    C. 15-17
    D. 16-18

2. Ladies League Baseball debuted in 1997 after the success of which film?

    A. The Sandlot
    B. A League of Their Own
    C. Field of Dreams
    D. Major League

3. The Continental League of Professional Baseball Clubs, or CL, was announced in 1959. It played how many games before folding?

    A. Zero
    B. One
    C. Two
    D. Three

4. The National Association of Base Ball Players was born in 1857, eliminating what era of baseball?

    A. Gotham era
    B. Knickerbocker era
    C. Amateur era
    D. Professional era

5. Only one current team survived the NABBP. Which team is it?

    A. Chicago Cubs
    B. Chicago White Sox
    C. Boston Red Sox

D. San Francisco Giants

6. The Federal League of Base Ball Clubs, or Federal League, completed three seasons. Which team won the first two?

    A. Cleveland Green Sox
    B. St. Louis Terriers
    C. Chicago Keeleys
    D. Indianapolis Hoosiers

7. The Players' National League of Professional Base Ball Clubs lasted one season, with which team coming in last place?

    A. Pittsburgh Burghers
    B. Chicago Pirates
    C. Buffalo Bisons
    D. Cleveland Infants

8. The United Baseball League was formed in 1994 but didn't play. Which of these teams was not announced by the league?

    A. Vancouver
    B. New Orleans
    C. Cuba
    D. Puerto Rico

9. The United States Baseball League played one partial season in 1912. Who won it?

    A. Cincinnati Cams
    B. Pittsburgh Filipinos
    C. Richmond Rebels
    D. Cleveland Forest City

10. True or False: The American League joined the National League in 1901, with ten teams of their own.

11. True or False: The Cleveland Bluebirds were previously named the Cleveland Lake Shores.

12. The first change to the American League in decades came in 1961, when two teams were added by expansion. How many years did the league wait to add teams to the National League?

    A. One
    B. Two

C. Three
D. Four

13. True or False: Division play in the MLB began in 1968, with each league split into two divisions.

14. The MLB expanded in 1977 once more, again with the American League adding two teams. How many years did it take for the National League to add two more teams of their own?

    A. 12
    B. 16
    C. 18
    D. 20

15. One year after the expansion in 1993, MLB realigned the divisions, splitting each league into how many divisions?

    A. Three
    B. Four
    C. Five
    D. Six

16. True or False: The next expansion in 1998 finally added one team to each league.

17. The leagues' divisions finally became equal when which team switched leagues in 2013?

    A. Minnesota Twins
    B. Milwaukee Brewers
    C. Houston Astros
    D. Arizona Diamondbacks

18. True or False: Four of the 12 National League teams folded after the 1899 season.

CHAPTER 16 ANSWERS:

1. D. 16-18. The league was discontinued in 2016.
2. B. A League of Their Own. This league lasted two seasons before folding.
3. A. Zero. The league did not play but secured negotiations with MLB to expand.
4. B. Knickerbocker era. This association established common rules and standards to eliminate match-fixing and other issues of the time.
5. A. Chicago Cubs. They played their first season in 1870 as the Chicago White Stockings.
6. D. Indianapolis Hoosiers. The Hoosiers finished one game ahead of the Chicago Generals in 1914.
7. C. Buffalo Bisons. They finished 46 and ½ games back from the Boston Reds.
8. C. Cuba. The league folded, citing stadium problems.
9. B. Pittsburgh Filipinos. The league was seen as a precursor to the Federal League.
10. False. The American League only had eight teams, matching the NL.
11. True. Today, they are the Cleveland Guardians after more than 100 years as the Indians.
12. A. 1. The NL added two squads in 1962.
13. False. Divisional play began in 1969.
14. B. 16. The NL added two more squads in 1993.
15. A. Three. The West division of each league had one fewer team than the other divisions.
16. True. Arizona joined the NL, and Tampa joined the AL.
17. C. Houston Astros. It would solidify the divisions and leagues to the present day.
18. True. It made the league stronger in the long run.

DID YOU KNOW?

The Brooklyn Dodgers were known as the Brooklyn Trolley Dodgers for two years.

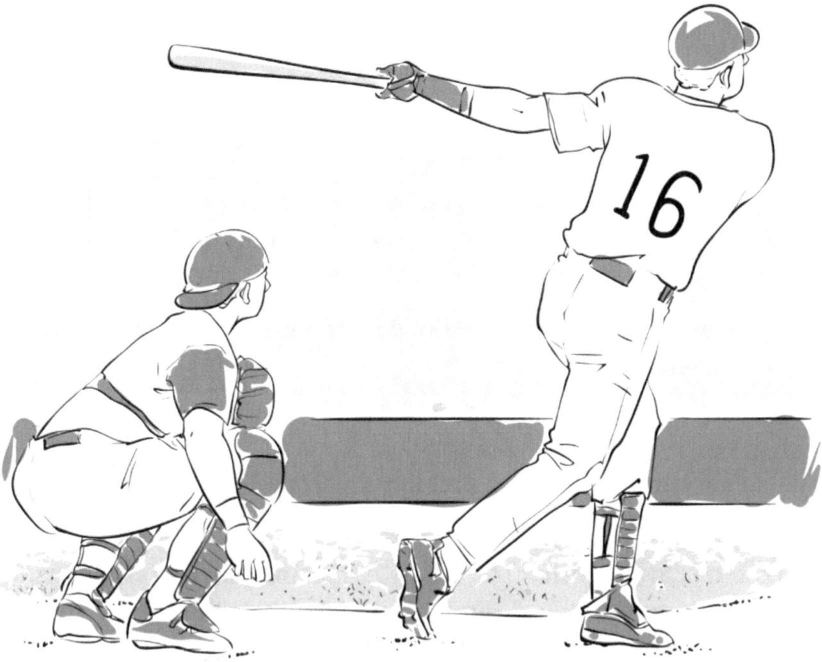
16

CHAPTER 17:
THE AMERICAN LEAGUE

1. True or False: The American League has won the World Series 68 times since 1903.

2. Which team has won more AL pennants than any other?
   A. New York Yankees
   B. Boston Red Sox
   C. Philadelphia Athletics
   D. Detroit Tigers

3. True or False: The American League, until 2022, was the only league that allowed a designated hitter.

4. Until the late 1970s, how did AL umpires dress differently from NL umpires?
   A. They wore blue instead of black.
   B. They wore white instead of black.
   C. They wore their chest protector over their coat.
   D. They wore their chest protector under their coat.

5. True or False: Until 2022, when AL teams played NL teams, they would only use the designated hitter when they were the home team.

6. The American League was considered an independent entity until what year, when it officially merged with the NL under the umbrella of Major League Baseball?
   A. 1991
   B. 1996
   C. 2000
   D. 2002

7. True or False: The American League began with eight charter teams for the first 43 years of their existence.

8. The Boston Americans became which team in 1908, seven years after the AL's formation?

   A. Boston Red Sox
   B. Boston Beanhoppers
   C. Boston Braves
   D. Boston Bruins

9. True or False: The Detroit Tigers have not changed their city or name since 1894.

10. Though it is vacant as of 2023, who most recently held the honorary position of American League President?

    A. Jackie Autry
    B. Frank Robinson
    C. Gene Budig
    D. Bobby Brown

11. True or False: The New York Highlanders were so named by the press because of their stadium's name, Hilltop Park.

12. The Cleveland Naps were so named in honor of which MLB Hall of Fame player?

    A. Napoleon Lajoie
    B. Cy Young
    C. Addie Joss
    D. Shoeless Joe Jackson

13. True or False: The Current AL Central has more teams from before 1900 than any other AL division.

14. The Chicago White Sox were enfranchised as which team in 1894?

    A. Sioux City Cornhuskers
    B. Grand Rapids Rippers
    C. Kansas City Blues
    D. Minneapolis Millers

15. True or False: The Cleveland Guardians were known as the Grand Rapids Furniture Makers in 1899.

16. Which of these names was first used by the franchise now known as the Minnesota Twins?

    A. Washington Nationals

B. Kansas City Blues
C. Kansas City Cowboys
D. Washington Senators

17. True or False: The Toronto Blue Jays won two World Series titles back-to-back in the early 1990s.

18. How many division titles have the Seattle Mariners won?
    A. One
    B. Two
    C. Three
    D. Four

CHAPTER 17 ANSWERS:

1. True. It has been contested 119 times, giving the AL a slight edge.
2. A. New York Yankees. They have won 40 pennants.
3. True. The National League would make their pitchers bat.
4. C. AL umps used to wear the protector over their uniforms, but now all umps wear it under their uniforms.
5. True. This was changed when both leagues adopted the designated hitter rule.
6. C. 2000. It didn't affect play but made each league more like conferences in other American sports.
7. False. The eight teams of the AL remained that way for 52 years.
8. A. Boston Red Sox. The rest is history.
9. True. They are one of the few teams to be steady with their name and location.
10. B. Frank Robinson. He stepped down from the honorary position in 2019.
11. True. Though, the name did not stick.
12. A. Napoleon Lajoie. His nickname was Nap.
13. True. Four of the five teams were enfranchised before 1900.
14. A. Sioux City Cornhuskers. They moved to St. Paul before going to Chicago in 1900.
15. True. The name only lasted one year before they moved to Cleveland in 1900.
16. C. Kansas City Cowboys. It was the team's name in 1894.
17. True. They have won the AL East six times.
18. C. Three. They also have two wild card berths, but no AL pennants.

DID YOU KNOW?

The Milwaukee Brewers only won one AL pennant, back in 1982.

CHAPTER 18:
THE NATIONAL LEAGUE

1. The National League is sometimes called what?

   A. Senior Circuit
   B. Junior Circuit
   C. Big Brother
   D. Little Brother

2. The National League was born with eight teams, but how many survived past the first season?

   A. Four
   B. Five
   C. Six
   D. Seven

3. How many of the remaining original National League teams folded after the second season?

   A. One
   B. Two
   C. Three
   D. Four

4. Two original National League teams from 1876 are still playing today. The Boston Red Stockings of 1876 exist as which current team?

   A. Boston Red Sox
   B. Atlanta Braves
   C. St. Louis Cardinals
   D. Cincinnati Reds

5. The Chicago White Stockings of 1876 exist as which current MLB team?

   A. Chicago White Sox
   B. Philadelphia Phillies

C. New York Mets
   D. Chicago Cubs

6. An 1894 game in which city ended in tragedy when fans started a fire in the stands, which spread and destroyed or damaged 100 buildings?

   A. Boston
   B. Baltimore
   C. New York
   D. Philadelphia

7. In 1962, the National League added two teams. The New York Mets was one, but what was the other?

   A. Milwaukee Brewers
   B. Colorado Rockies
   C. Florida Marlins
   D. Houston Colt .45s

8. When the league expanded in 1993, which of these teams did they add?

   A. Houston Astros
   B. Florida Marlins
   C. Arizona Diamondbacks
   D. Milwaukee Brewers

9. The NLCS was added to the MLB postseason in which year?

   A. 1966
   B. 1969
   C. 1976
   D. 1991

10. When did the NLCS and ALCS go from a five-game series to a seven-game series?

    A. 1981
    B. 1985
    C. 1990
    D. 1993

11. Which former National League President shares his name with the NLCS trophy?

A. William Hulbert
   B. Chub Feeney
   C. Warren Giles
   D. John Heydler

12. Who have the Cincinnati Reds beaten four times in the NLCS?

    A. Los Angeles Dodgers
    B. Philadelphia Phillies
    C. San Francisco Giants
    D. Pittsburgh Pirates

13. Which National League team has won the most NLCS titles but is also tied for the most NLCS losses?

    A. Los Angeles Dodgers
    B. St. Louis Cardinals
    C. Atlanta Braves
    D. Philadelphia Phillies

14. Besides the Rockies and Marlins, who have not lost in the NLCS, which team has the best NLCS winning percentage with five wins and two losses?

    A. St. Louis Cardinals
    B. Atlanta Braves
    C. Philadelphia Phillies
    D. San Francisco Giants

15. Only one National League team has yet to win the NLCS. Which team is it?

    A. Washington Nationals
    B. Milwaukee Brewers
    C. Houston Astros
    D. Chicago Cubs

16. What year did the Milwaukee Brewers move to the National League?

    A. 1995
    B. 1996
    C. 1997
    D. 1998

17. What year did the Houston Astros move away from the NL to the AL?

    A. 2012
    B. 2013
    C. 2014
    D. 2015

18. In 2005, the Montreal Expos moved and became which NL team?

    A. Washington Nationals
    B. San Diego Padres
    C. Miami Marlins
    D. Arizona Diamondbacks

CHAPTER 18 ANSWERS:

1. A. Senior Circuit. It was around for 25 years before the American League.
2. C. Six. Two teams were expelled after the first season.
3. C. Three. Another team would disband two years later, leaving only two founding teams.
4. B. Atlanta Braves. The team moved to Milwaukee, then to Atlanta.
5. D. Chicago Cubs. The Current White Sox have a different origin.
6. A. Boston. It was a terrible moment for the league.
7. D. Houston Colt .45s. They were renamed the Astros three years later.
8. B. Florida Marlins. They changed to Miami beginning with the 2012 season.
9. B. 1969. The division split made it necessary.
10. B. 1985. They are played in a 2-3-2 format.
11. C. Warren Giles. He was President of the National League from 1951 to 1969.
12. D. Pittsburgh Pirates. Their last meeting was in 1990.
13. A. Los Angeles Dodgers. They have won eight and lost seven.
14. D. San Francisco Giants. Their most recent NLCS win was in 2014.
15. B. Milwaukee Brewers. They have lost twice, most recently in 2018.
16. D. 1998. The MLB was not done with moving teams to even the leagues.
17. B. 2013. It would work out well for that franchise.
18. A. Washington Nationals. It was another name borrowed from the city's past.

DID YOU KNOW?

The League President role was eliminated in 1999 when the two leagues officially became one business entity.

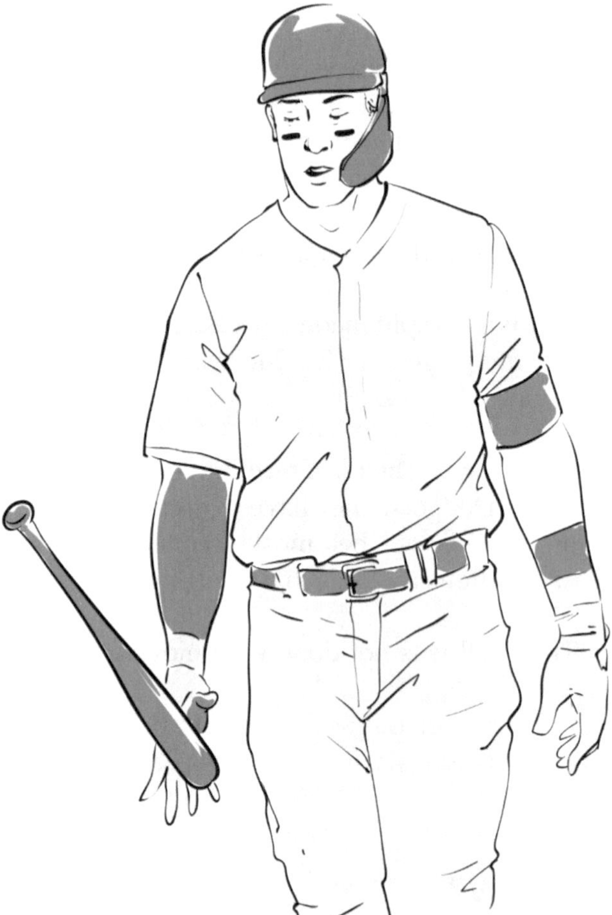

CHAPTER 19:

AL EAST

1. During the first 50 years of the AL East's existence, how many times did one of those teams reach the World Series?

    A. 22
    B. 27
    C. 33
    D. 39

2. Three of the current AL East teams have been there since the beginning. Those teams are the Red Sox, Yankees, and which team?

    A. Rays
    B. Blue Jays
    C. Orioles
    D. Tigers

3. The Yankees have 20 division titles, but how many each do the Orioles and Red Sox have?

    A. Ten
    B. 11
    C. 12
    D. 13

4. Which New York Yankees player leads the team in all-time games played?

    A. Yogi Berra
    B. Lou Gehrig
    C. Mickey Mantle
    D. Derek Jeter

5. Which Yankees pitcher leads the team in all-time wins?

    A. Whitey Ford
    B. Red Ruffing

C. Andy Pettitte
   D. Lefty Gomez

6. Which Yankees player leads the team in all-time RBIs?
   A. Babe Ruth
   B. Lou Gehrig
   C. Joe DiMaggio
   D. Mickey Mantle

7. Who leads the Boston Red Sox in all-time games played?
   A. Dwight Evans
   B. Ted Williams
   C. Carl Yastrzemski
   D. Jim Rice

8. Who leads the Red Sox in all-time home runs hit?
   A. Ted Williams
   B. David Ortiz
   C. Carl Yastrzemski
   D. Jim Rice

9. Cy Young is tied with which Red Sox pitcher for the most wins all-time for the team?
   A. Tim Wakefield
   B. Luis Tiant
   C. Mel Parnell
   D. Roger Clemens

10. Which Baltimore Oriole has played more games for the team than any other?
    A. Mark Belanger
    B. Brooks Robinson
    C. Cal Ripken Jr.
    D. Eddie Murray

11. Which Orioles pitcher has won 268 games, the most in team history?
    A. Jim Palmer
    B. Dave McNally
    C. Mike Mussina
    D. Mike Cuellar

12. Which Orioles pitcher collected 160 saves in six seasons, the most in team history?

    A. Zack Britton
    B. Jim Johnson
    C. Tippy Martinez
    D. Gregg Olson

13. Which Blue Jays player has hit the most home runs in the team's history?

    A. Jose Bautista
    B. Edwin Encarnacion
    C. Carlos Delgado
    D. Vernon Wells

14. Which Blue Jays player has worn the team's jersey in more games than any other?

    A. Carlos Delgado
    B. Tony Fernandez
    C. Vernon Wells
    D. Lloyd Moseby

15. Which Blue Jays pitcher has more wins than any other?

    A. Dave Stieb
    B. Roy Halladay
    C. Jim Clancy
    D. Jimmy Key

16. Which Tampa Bay Rays player has played more games for the team than anyone else?

    A. Carl Crawford
    B. Evan Longoria
    C. Ben Zobrist
    D. B.J. Upton

17. Which Rays pitcher is the team's all-time leader in wins?

    A. David Price
    B. Chris Archer
    C. Scott Kazmir
    D. James Shields

18. Which Rays pitcher leads the team in saves?
    A. Alex Colome
    B. Fernando Rodney
    C. Roberto Hernandez
    D. Danys Baez

CHAPTER 19 ANSWERS:

1. B. 27. It was substantially more than any other AL division.
2. C. Orioles. They were a founding member.
3. A. Ten. The Red Sox won most recently in 2018, the Orioles in 2023.
4. D. Derek Jeter. He played 2747 games, over 300 more than Mantle, who is second all-time.
5. A. Whitey Ford. He won 236 games with the Yankees.
6. B. Lou Gehrig. He hit 1995 RBIs, 24 more than Babe Ruth.
7. C. Carl Yastrzemski. He has the next player beat by more than 800 games.
8. A. Ted Williams. He's hit 521 of them.
9. D. Roger Clemens. They've both won 192 games.
10. C. Cal Ripkin Jr. He has played 105 more games than Robinson.
11. A. Jim Palmer. He has 87 more wins than McNally.
12. D. Gregg Olson. He has 21 more than Britton, in two fewer seasons.
13. C. Carlos Delgado. He hit 336 home runs.
14. B. Tony Fernandez. He played 27 more games than Delgado.
15. A. Dave Stieb. He gathered 175 wins over 15 seasons with the team.
16. B. Evan Longoria. He played 1435 games for Tampa.
17. D. James Shields. He won 87 games for the Rays.
18. C. Roberto Hernandez. He collected 101 saves in only three seasons for the team.

DID YOU KNOW?

The AL East is considered to be the toughest in baseball, based on their success over the years.

CHAPTER 20:
AL CENTRAL

1. This division formed when the AL East and AL West were split. What year did this division begin?

    A. 1992
    B. 1993
    C. 1994
    D. 1995

2. Which AL Central team joined after the Brewers left for the NL Central in 1998?

    A. Kansas City Royals
    B. Detroit Tigers
    C. Minnesota Twins
    D. Chicago White Sox

3. Which AL Central team has won the most division titles?

    A. Minnesota Twins
    B. Chicago White Sox
    C. Detroit Tigers
    D. Cleveland Guardians

4. Which Cleveland Guardian has played the most games for the franchise?

    A. Terry Turner
    B. Nap Lajoie
    C. Lou Boudreau
    D. Jim Hegan

5. Which Cleveland Guardian is the team's all-time leader in home runs?

    A. Albert Belle
    B. Manny Ramirez
    C. Jim Thome

D. Earl Averill

6. Which Guardians pitcher won 266 games in his career, the most all-time for the team?

    A. Bob Feller
    B. Mel Harder
    C. Bob Lemon
    D. Stan Coveleski

7. Which Chicago White Sox slugger leads the franchise in home runs?

    A. Paul Konerko
    B. Jose Abreu
    C. Frank Thomas
    D. Harold Baines

8. Which White Sox player leads the franchise in games played?

    A. Frank Thomas
    B. Nellie Fox
    C. Paul Konerko
    D. Luke Appling

9. Which White Sox pitcher has more wins for the franchise than any other?

    A. Ted Lyons
    B. Red Faber
    C. Ed Walsh
    D. Billy Pierce

10. Which Minnesota Twins player leads the franchise with 559 home runs?

    A. Harmon Killebrew
    B. Kent Hrbek
    C. Bob Allison
    D. Justin Morneau

11. Which Minnesota Twin has scored more runs than any other player in franchise history?

    A. Harmon Killebrew
    B. Sam Rice

C. Joe Judge
D. Kirby Puckett

12. Which Twins pitcher leads the organization in all-time wins?

    A. Bert Blyleven
    B. Jim Kaat
    C. Walter Johnson
    D. Brad Radke

13. Which Kansas City Royals player is the organization's all-time leader in runs scored, home runs, and RBIs?

    A. Hal McRae
    B. Amos Otis
    C. George Brett
    D. Frank White

14. Which Royals pitcher spent his entire 15-year career with the team, collecting 166 wins in the process to lead the organization?

    A. Kevin Appier
    B. Mark Gubicza
    C. Dennis Leonard
    D. Paul Splittorff

15. Which Royals' pitcher is the organization's all-time leader in saves, with 304?

    A. Jeff Montgomery
    B. Dan Quisenberry
    C. Joakim Soria
    D. Greg Holland

16. Who is the Detroit Tigers' all-time leader in home runs?

    A. Miguel Cabrera
    B. Al Kaline
    C. Norm Cash
    D. Hank Greenberg

17. Which Tigers player, now in the Hall of Fame, is the organization's all-time leader in RBIs?

    A. Ty Cobb
    B. Al Kaline

C. Harry Heilmann
   D. Charlie Gehringer

18. Which Tigers pitcher from the 1910s and 1920s won 223 games for the team, the most all-time for the organization?
    A. Hooks Dauss
    B. George Mullin
    C. Mickey Lolich
    D. Hal Newhouser

CHAPTER 20 ANSWERS:

1. C. 1994. Three AL West teams and two AL East teams formed the division.
2. B. Detroit Tigers. They came from the AL East.
3. D. Cleveland Guardians. They have won 11 division titles.
4. A. Terry Turner. He played five more games than Nap Lajoie.
5. C. Jim Thome. He hit 337 home runs for the team.
6. A. Bob Feller. In 18 seasons, he won 266 games.
7. C. Frank Thomas. He hit 448 home runs for the team.
8. D. Luke Appling. He played 2,422 games for the franchise.
9. A. Ted Lyons. He won 260 games in 21 years for the franchise.
10. A. Harmon Killebrew. The next closest Twin has 293 home runs.
11. B. Sam Rice. He scored 1466 runs in 19 seasons with the team.
12. C. Walter Johnson. In 21 seasons, he notched 417 wins.
13. C. George Brett. He is a Hall of Fame player.
14. D. Paul Splittorff. He retired from the game in 1984.
15. A. Jeff Montgomery. He played 12 seasons with the team.
16. B. Al Kaline. He fell one short of 400 home runs.
17. A. Ty Cobb. He collected 1,811 RBIs in 22 years.
18. A. Hooks Dauss. He won those 223 games over 15 seasons.

DID YOU KNOW?

The AL Central has been won by the Guardians 11 times.

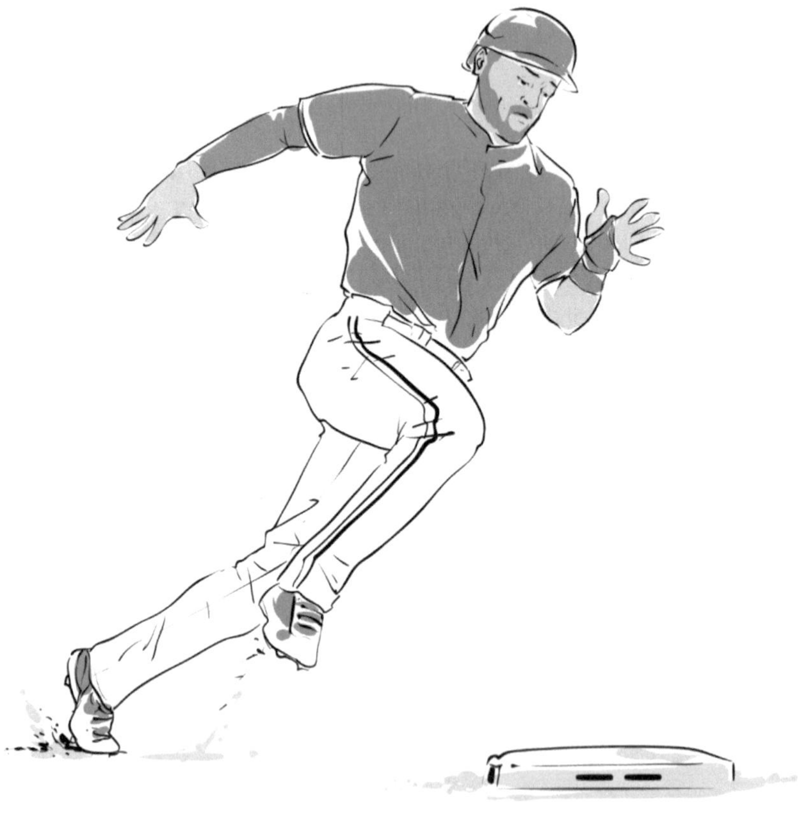

CHAPTER 21:

AL WEST

1. Throughout its history, which AL West team was geographically the furthest east?

   A. Chicago White Sox
   B. Milwaukee Brewers
   C. Minnesota Twins
   D. Kansas City Royals

2. From 1998 to 2012, the AL West was the only division with how many teams?

   A. Seven
   B. Six
   C. Five
   D. Four

3. Which team has won the most AL West titles since it was founded in 1969?

   A. Houston Astros
   B. Oakland Athletics
   C. Texas Rangers
   D. Los Angeles Angels

4. Which Los Angeles Angels player has hit more home runs for the organization than any other?

   A. Tim Salmon
   B. Garret Anderson
   C. Mike Trout
   D. Brian Downing

5. No Angels player has played in more games than which player, who played 15 seasons with the team?

   A. Garret Anderson
   B. Tim Salmon

C. Brian Downing
   D. Mike Trout

6. Which Angels pitcher has amassed more wins for the organization than any other?

   A. Jered Weaver
   B. Nolan Ryan
   C. Chuck Finley
   D. Mike Witt

7. Which Hall-of-Fame player has hit more home runs for the Houston Astros than any other player?

   A. Lance Berkman
   B. Craig Biggio
   C. Jim Wynn
   D. Jeff Bagwell

8. Which Astros pitcher has won more games than any other pitcher in the organization?

   A. Roy Oswalt
   B. Joe Niekro
   C. Larry Dierker
   D. Mike Scott

9. Which Astros player has worn the team's jersey for more games than any other player?

   A. Jose Altuve
   B. Jose Cruz
   C. Jeff Bagwell
   D. Craig Biggio

10. Which player is not in the Hall of Fame but has played more games for the Oakland Athletics than any other player in history?

    A. Rickey Henderson
    B. Jimmy Dykes
    C. Sal Bando
    D. Bert Campaneris

11. Which Oakland Athletics player has hit more homers for the organization than any other?

A. Mark McGwire
   B. Jimmie Foxx
   C. Reggie Jackson
   D. Jose Canseco

12. Which Astros pitcher is in the Hall of Fame and won more games for the organization than any other pitcher?

    A. Lefty Grove
    B. Charles Bender
    C. Eddie Plank
    D. Eddie Rommel

13. Which Seattle Mariner is the only one to have played more than 2,000 games with the club?

    A. Ichiro Suzuki
    B. Edgar Martinez
    C. Ken Griffey Jr.
    D. Kyle Seager

14. Which Mariner is in the Hall of Fame and also leads the organization in home runs?

    A. Edgar Martinez
    B. Jay Buhner
    C. Kyle Seager
    D. Ken Griffey Jr.

15. Which Mariners pitcher played his entire career with the team and leads them in career wins?

    A. Randy Johnson
    B. Felix Hernandez
    C. Jamie Moyer
    D. Freddy Garcia

16. Which Texas Rangers player has played over 1,800 games for the organization?

    A. Michael Young
    B. Elvis Andrus
    C. Rafael Palmeiro
    D. Jim Sundberg

17. Which Ranger leads the organization in home runs and played 13 years for the team, ending in 2003?

    A. Ivan Rodriguez
    B. Rafael Palmeiro
    C. Juan Gonzalez
    D. Frank Howard

18. The Rangers have three pitchers in team history with more than 100 wins. Which pitcher leads the pack with 139 wins?

    A. Charlie Hough
    B. Kenny Rogers
    C. Bobby Witt
    D. Fergie Jenkins

CHAPTER 21 ANSWERS:

1. A. Chicago White Sox. They left to join the AL Central in 1994.
2. D. Four. The NL West expanded to five in 1998.
3. B. Oakland Athletics. They have won 17 titles over the history of the division.
4. C. Mike Trout. He hit 368 home runs over 13 seasons.
5. A. Garret Anderson. He played 2,013 games.
6. C. Chuck Finley. He collected 165 wins in 14 seasons.
7. D. Jeff Bagwell. He hit 449 homers over 15 seasons.
8. B. Joe Niekro. He won 144 games, one more than Roy Oswalt.
9. D. Craig Biggio. He played 2,850 games over 20 years.
10. D. Bert Campaneris. He played 1,795 games with the team over 13 years.
11. A. Mark McGwire. He hit 363 home runs for the organization over 12 years.
12. C. Eddie Plank. He won 284 games for the team over 14 years.
13. B. Edgar Martinez. He played 2,055 games in 18 seasons.
14. D. Ken Griffey Jr. He hit 417 home runs over 13 seasons.
15. B. Felix Hernandez. He won 169 games over 15 seasons.
16. A. Michael Young. The next closest Ranger has not played 1,700 games.
17. C. Juan Gonzalez. He hit 372 home runs.
18. A. Charlie Hough. He played 11 seasons with the team.

DID YOU KNOW?

The Oakland Athletics won the AL West title five times in a row, from 1971 to 1975.

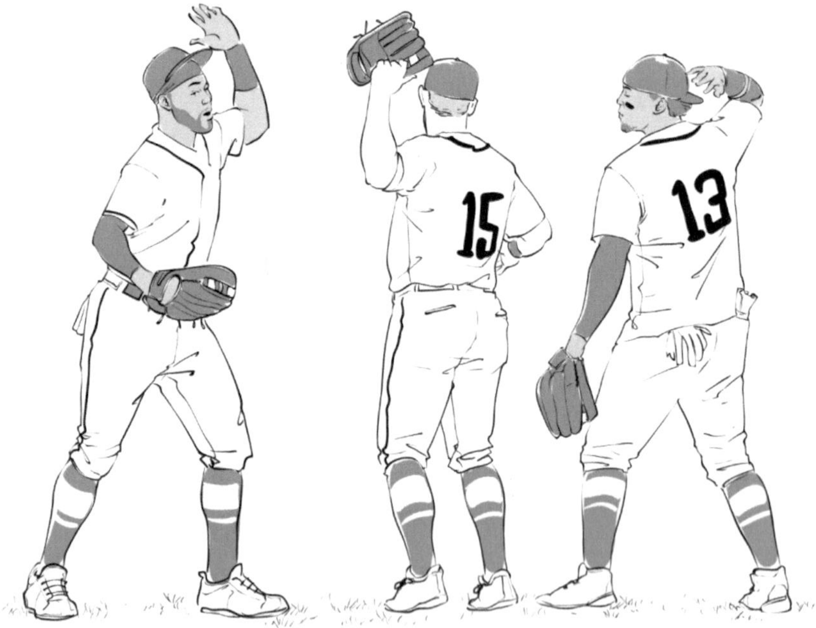
15
13

CHAPTER 22:
NL EAST

1. Out of the current NL East teams, which one joined most recently?

   A. Miami Marlins
   B. Washington Nationals
   C. New York Mets
   D. Atlanta Braves

2. Which team won 11 straight NL East titles?

   A. Philadelphia Phillies
   B. Atlanta Braves
   C. New York Mets
   D. Pittsburgh Pirates

3. In the NL East's first year, which NL East team won the World Series?

   A. Pittsburgh Pirates
   B. New York Mets
   C. Philadelphia Phillies
   D. Montreal Expos

4. Which New York Mets player has played over 1,800 games for the team?

   A. David Wright
   B. Jose Reyes
   C. Ed Kranepool
   D. Bud Harrelson

5. Only three Mets have hit more than 200 home runs. Which player has the most?

   A. David Wright
   B. Mike Piazza
   C. Howard Johnson
   D. Darryl Strawberry

6. Which pitcher is in the Hall of Fame and won 198 games with the Mets?

   A. Tom Seaver
   B. Dwight Gooden
   C. Jerry Koosman
   D. Ron Darling

7. Which Phillies player played 2,404 games with the team on his way to the Hall of Fame?

   A. Jimmy Rollins
   B. Richie Ashburn
   C. Larry Bowa
   D. Mike Schmidt

8. Which Phillies slugger amassed 2,306 hits over 15 years with the team?

   A. Ed Delahanty
   B. Jimmy Rollins
   C. Mike Schmidt
   D. Richie Ashburn

9. Which Phillies pitcher has the most wins for the franchise?

   A. Robin Roberts
   B. Steve Carlton
   C. Grover Alexander
   D. Chris Short

10. Which player played 3,076 games for the organization known today as the Atlanta Braves?

    A. Chipper Jones
    B. Eddie Mathews
    C. Henry Aaron
    D. Dale Murphy

11. Which pitcher won 356 games for the Braves organization?

    A. Warren Spahn
    B. Kid Nichols
    C. Phil Nierko
    D. Tom Glavine

12. Which pitcher leads the Braves in saves all time but only played five seasons with them?

    A. Gene Garber
    B. John Smoltz
    C. Mark Wohlers
    D. Craig Kimbrel

13. The Miami Marlins have two players with more than 1,000 games played. Who has the most?

    A. Luis Castillo
    B. Jeff Conine
    C. Giancarlo Stanton
    D. Mike Lowell

14. Only one Marlins player has hit more than 200 home runs for the organization. Who was it?

    A. Dan Uggla
    B. Hanley Ramirez
    C. Giancarlo Stanton
    D. Mike Lowell

15. Only two Marlins pitchers have notched over 100 saves. Who has the most?

    A. Robb Nen
    B. Antonio Alfonseca
    C. Steve Cishek
    D. AJ Ramos

16. Five Washington Nationals have played more than 1,400 games with the organization. Three of them are Hall of Famers. Which Nationals player has played the most games for the franchise?

    A. Gary Carter
    B. Tim Raines
    C. Ryan Zimmerman
    D. Andre Dawson

17. Which pitcher, for the team now called the Nationals, won 158 games from 1973 to 1985?

    A. Stephen Strasburg
    B. Dennis Martinez

C. Max Scherzer
D. Steve Rogers

18. Six pitchers from the organization now located in Washington have earned more than 100 saves. Who collected 152, the most of anyone in the organization?

    A. Chad Cordero
    B. Jeff Reardon
    C. Ugueth Urbina
    D. Mel Rojas

CHAPTER 22 ANSWERS:

1. D. Atlanta Braves. They joined in 1994 from the NL West.
2. B. Atlanta Braves. They are also on a six-year streak as of 2023.
3. B. New York Mets. They beat the Orioles in 1969.
4. C. Ed Kranepool. The next closest player didn't play more than 1,600 games.
5. D. Darryl Strawberry. He hit 252 home runs for the Mets.
6. A. Tom Seaver. He played 12 years with the team.
7. D. Mike Schmidt. He is one of two players to have more than 2,000 games with the organization.
8. B. Jimmy Rollins. His final year with the team was in 2014.
9. B. Steve Carlton. He won 241 games.
10. C. Henry Aaron. He also hit 733 home runs!
11. A. Warren Spahn. He played 20 years for the team.
12. D. Craig Kimbrel. He collected 186 saves.
13. A. Luis Castillo. He played 1,128 games in ten years.
14. C. Giancarlo Stanton. He collected 267 homers over eight seasons.
15. A. Robb Nen. He played five years for the Marlins.
16. C. Ryan Zimmerman. He played 1799 games for the team.
17. D. Steve Rogers. He also lost 152 games.
18. B. Jeff Reardon. He played six seasons from 1981 to 1986.

DID YOU KNOW?

Each team from the NL East has won a World Series title.

CHAPTER 23:
NL CENTRAL

1. When the NL Central was created, which team was supposed to stay in the NL East, but plans changed?

    A. St. Louis Cardinals
    B. Cincinnati Reds
    C. Pittsburgh Pirates
    D. Milwaukee Brewers

2. Which NL Central team dominated the first 26 years of the division's existence, winning 12 division crowns?

    A. Chicago Cubs
    B. Cincinnati Reds
    C. Pittsburgh Pirates
    D. St. Louis Cardinals

3. Which member of the NL Central had not won the NL Central title as of 2023?

    A. Pittsburgh Pirates
    B. Cincinnati Reds
    C. Milwaukee Brewers
    D. Chicago Cubs

4. Two Pittsburgh Pirates are tied for the most games played for the organization. One is Honus Wagner. Who is the other?

    A. Willie Stargell
    B. Max Carey
    C. Roberto Clemente
    D. Bill Mazeroski

5. Which Pirates player has hit more home runs for the organization than any other player?

    A. Willie Stargell
    B. Ralph Kiner

C. Roberto Clemente
D. Andrew McCutchen

6. Which Pirates pitcher collected 202 wins in 13 years with the team?

    A. Babe Adams
    B. Wilbur Cooper
    C. Sam Leever
    D. Bob Friend

7. Only one Chicago Cubs pitcher has amassed more than 200 wins for the club. Who was it?

    A. Mordecai Brown
    B. Bill Hutchison
    C. Larry Corcoran
    D. Charlie Root

8. Which Cubs slugger leads the organization in home runs, though he's not (yet) in the Hall of Fame?

    A. Sammy Sosa
    B. Ernie Banks
    C. Billy Williams
    D. Ron Santo

9. Which Chicago Cub played all 19 years of his career with the team and has played more games for the organization than anyone else?

    A. Cap Anson
    B. Billy Williams
    C. Ernie Banks
    D. Ryne Sandberg

10. In 19 years with the Cincinnati Reds, which player leads the organization in all-time games played?

    A. Dave Concepcion
    B. Pete Rose
    C. Barry Larkin
    D. Johnny Bench

11. Three Reds have hit more than 300 career home runs. As of 2023, who has hit the most?

A. Joey Votto
B. Frank Robinson
C. Tony Perez
D. Johnny Bench

12. Which Reds pitcher is the only one to have collected more than 170 wins, back in the 1920s and 30s?

    A. Eppa Rixey
    B. Tony Mullane
    C. Paul Derringer
    D. Bucky Walters

13. Which Milwaukee Brewers player has played 1,000 more games than any other player in the organization?

    A. Paul Molitor
    B. Jim Gantner
    C. Robin Yount
    D. Ryan Braun

14. Which Brewers player has hit 101 more home runs than any other player in the organization?

    A. Ryan Braun
    B. Robin Yount
    C. Prince Fielder
    D. Geoff Jenkins

15. Only two Brewers pitchers have amassed more than 100 wins. Who has the most?

    A. Mike Caldwell
    B. Teddy Higuera
    C. Moose Haas
    D. Jim Slaton

16. Which St. Louis Cardinals great played 700+ more games than any other in the organization?

    A. Lou Brock
    B. Stan Musial
    C. Yadier Molina
    D. Ozzie Smith

17. Which Cardinals pitcher has won more games than any other pitcher in the organization?

    A. Bob Gibson
    B. Jesse Haines
    C. Adam Wainwright
    D. Bob Forsch

18. Only one Cardinals pitcher has more than 200 saves. Who?

    A. Lee Smith
    B. Todd Worrell
    C. Jason Isringhausen
    D. Bruce Sutter

CHAPTER 23 ANSWERS:

1. C. Pittsburgh Pirates. The Braves wanted to stay in the NL East to form a rivalry with the new Florida Marlins.
2. D. St. Louis Cardinals. They have won three in a row, twice.
3. A. Pittsburgh Pirates. Their last division title was in 1992 before the NL Central existed.
4. C. Roberto Clemente. They both played 2,433 games for the Pirates organization.
5. A. Willie Stargell. He hit 475 in 21 years.
6. B. Wilbur Cooper. He won eight more games than Babe Adams.
7. D. Charlie Root. His 201 wins are 13 ahead of Mordecai Brown.
8. A. Sammy Sosa. He hit 545 home runs in 13 years with the team.
9. C. Ernie Banks. He finished his career in 1971.
10. B. Pete Rose. He played 2,722 games.
11. D. Johnny Bench. He hit 389 home runs in 17 seasons.
12. A. Eppa Rixey. He played 13 seasons with the team, winning 179 games.
13. C. Robin Yount. He played 2,856 games in 20 seasons.
14. A. Ryan Braun. He hit 352 home runs in 14 seasons.
15. D. Jim Slaton. He won 117 games in 12 seasons with the team.
16. B. Stan Musial. He played 3,026 games in 22 seasons with the team.
17. A. Bob Gibson. He won 251 games over 17 seasons with the team.
18. C. Jason Isringhausen. He collected 217 saves in seven seasons.

DID YOU KNOW?

The Brewers were part of the AL West, East, and Central before moving to the NL Central.

CHAPTER 24:
NL WEST

1. Which team dominated the NL West from 2013 to 2023, winning ten of 11 division titles?

   A. San Francisco Giants
   B. Arizona Diamondbacks
   C. Los Angeles Dodgers
   D. San Diego Padres

2. Which team joined the NL West in 1993 but has not won the division as of 2023?

   A. San Francisco Giants
   B. Arizona Diamondbacks
   C. San Diego Padres
   D. Colorado Rockies

3. Since 1969, how many World Series championships have been won by teams emerging from the NL West?

   A. Eight
   B. Nine
   C. Ten
   D. 11

4. Which Dodgers player appeared in more games for the team than anyone else?

   A. Bill Russell
   B. Pee Wee Reese
   C. Zack Wheat
   D. Gil Hodges

5. Which Dodgers player has hit more home runs for the organization than anyone else?

   A. Duke Snider
   B. Gil Hodges

C. Eric Karros
   D. Roy Campanella

6. Three Dodgers pitchers have more than 200 wins. Who has the most (as of 2023)?
   A. Clayton Kershaw
   B. Don Drysdale
   C. Dazzy Vance
   D. Don Sutton

7. Which player from the 1950s and 60s played more games for the Giants than anyone else?
   A. Mel Ott
   B. Willie Mays
   C. Willie McCovey
   D. Bill Terry

8. Mays also led the Giants in career home runs. How many HRs behind him was Barry Bonds?
   A. 60
   B. 70
   C. 80
   D. 90

9. Which pitcher leads the Giants with the most wins all time?
   A. Carl Hubbell
   B. Juan Marichal
   C. Mickey Welch
   D. Christy Mathewson

10. Which Diamondbacks player is the only one to have played more than 1,100 games for the team?
    A. Luis Gonzalez
    B. Paul Goldschmidt
    C. David Peralta
    D. Miguel Montero

11. Which Diamondbacks pitcher is the only one to have more than 100 wins for the organization?
    A. Brandon Webb
    B. Curt Schilling

C. Patrick Corbin
D. Randy Johnson

12. Only one Diamondbacks pitcher collected more than 90 saves. Who was it?

    A. J.J. Putz
    B. Matt Mantei
    C. Jose Valverde
    D. Byung-Hyun Kim

13. Only one Colorado Rockies player has played more than 2,200 games for the team. Who?

    A. Charlie Blackmon
    B. Carlos Gonzalez
    C. Todd Helton
    D. Larry Walker

14. Which Rockies pitcher has won more games for the team than any other player?

    A. Aaron Cook
    B. Jorge De La Rosa
    C. German Marquez
    D. Jeff Francis

15. Two Rockies pitchers have surpassed 100 saves. Who has the most?

    A. Jose Jimenez
    B. Huston Street
    C. Brian Fuentes
    D. Daniel Bard

16. Which San Diego Padres player leads the organization in all-time games played?

    A. Tony Gwynn
    B. Garry Templeton
    C. Dave Winfield
    D. Tim Flannery

17. Which Padre only played six seasons with the team but is the leader in all-time home runs for the squad?

A. Dave Winfield
B. Phil Nevin
C. Adrian Gonzalez
D. Nate Colbert

18. One Padres pitcher reached the 100-win plateau. Who was it?
    A. Randy Jones
    B. Eric Show
    C. Jake Peavy
    D. Ed Whitson

CHAPTER 24 ANSWERS:

1. C. Los Angeles Dodgers. The 2023 title was their 21st division title.
2. D. Colorado Rockies. In 2018, they lost a one-game playoff to the Dodgers for the title.
3. B. Nine. Most recently, the Dodgers won in 2020 over the Rays.
4. C. Zack Wheat. He played 2,322 games over 18 years.
5. A. Duke Snider. He hit 389 home runs over 16 seasons.
6. D. Don Sutton. Kershaw was 23 wins behind him as of 2023.
7. B. Willie Mays. He played 2,857 games over 21 seasons.
8. A. 60. Mays hit 646, Bonds hit 586.
9. D. Christy Mathewson. He won 372 games over 17 years.
10. A. Luis Gonzalez. He played 1,194 games over eight seasons.
11. D. Randy Johnson. He won 118 games over eight years.
12. C. Jose Valverde. He collected 98 saves over five years.
13. C. Todd Helton. He played 2,247 games over 17 seasons.
14. B. Jorge De La Rosa. He won 86 games over nine seasons.
15. C. Brian Fuentes. He earned 115 saves in seven seasons.
16. A. Tony Gwynn. He played 2,440 games over 20 years.
17. D. Nate Colbert. He hit 163 home runs in six seasons.
18. B. Eric Show. His 100 wins came over ten years.

DID YOU KNOW?

The Dodgers have won the division 21 times since its inception.

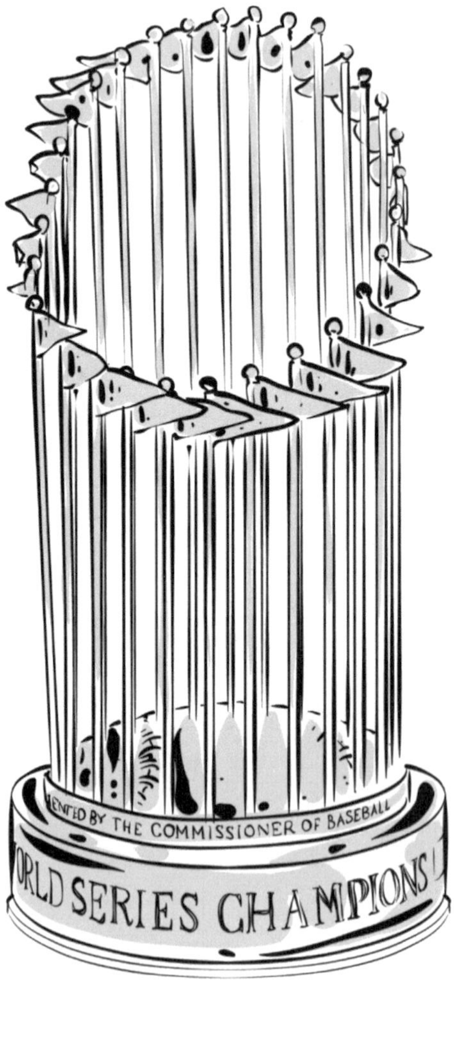
ENTED BY THE COMMISSIONER OF BASEBALL
ORLD SERIES CHAMPIONS

CHAPTER 25:
THE WORLD SERIES

1. The precursor to the World Series was not well organized. How many games did the 1887 iteration of the World Series take to decide a winner?

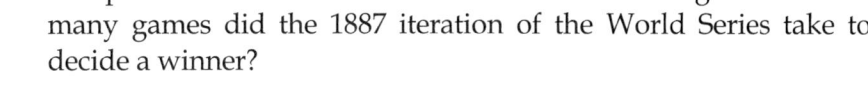

    A. Ten
    B. 12
    C. 15
    D. 17

2. The first modern World Series took place in what year?

    A. 1901
    B. 1902
    C. 1903
    D. 1904

3. When the World Series first came about, it had a different name. What was it?

    A. World's Championship Series
    B. World's Baseball Championship
    C. World Baseball Series
    D. World's Baseball Series

4. The White Sox purposely lost the 1919 World Series to which team?

    A. New York Giants
    B. Cincinnati Reds
    C. Chicago Cubs
    D. Pittsburgh Pirates

5. The Yankees bought Babe Ruth's contract in 1919. How many years later did they reach their first World Series?

    A. One
    B. Two

C. Three
D. Four

6. The first World Series to be broadcast on the radio happened in which year?

   A. 1920
   B. 1921
   C. 1922
   D. 1923

7. The first World Series game scheduled at night was Game 4 of the World Series during which year?

   A. 1946
   B. 1947
   C. 1948
   D. 1949

8. Carlton Fisk hit a game-winning home run in the 1975 World Series for which team?

   A. Boston Red Sox
   B. Cincinnati Reds
   C. New York Mets
   D. Los Angeles Dodgers

9. In the 1970s, three teams each won the World Series and successfully defended it at least once. Which of these teams did not take part in that unmatched streak?

   A. Oakland Athletics
   B. Pittsburgh Pirates
   C. New York Yankees
   D. Cincinnati Reds

10. Even though the AL added the designated hitter in 1973, the DH did not come to the World Series until which year?

    A. 1974
    B. 1975
    C. 1976
    D. 1977

11. The 1985 World Series had a controversial call that helped which team win Games 6 and 7?

A. Kansas City Royals
B. Detroit Tigers
C. St. Louis Cardinals
D. Cincinnati Reds

12. The 1986 Mets were down to their final out in Game 6, down two runs in the bottom of the tenth inning. They rallied to win Game 6, then Game 7, beating which team?

    A. New York Yankees
    B. Boston Red Sox
    C. Detroit Tigers
    D. Chicago White Sox

13. Which team was the first to win the World Series by winning all of their home games but losing all of their away games?

    A. Minnesota Twins
    B. St. Louis Cardinals
    C. Atlanta Braves
    D. Los Angeles Dodgers

14. Kirk Gibson hit a walk-off home run in Game 1 of the 1988 World Series, though he was noticeably injured. His Dodgers beat which team to win the championship?

    A. Boston Red Sox
    B. New York Yankees
    C. Detroit Tigers
    D. Oakland Athletics

15. The 1991 World Series went for seven games. How many were decided by one run?

    A. Three
    B. Four
    C. Five
    D. Six

16. The first World Series games played outside of the United States took place in this year.

    A. 1992
    B. 1993
    C. 1994
    D. 1995

17. True or False: The San Francisco Giants won the World Series in 2010, 2012, and 2014 but didn't make the playoffs in 2011 or 2013.

18. The Chicago Cubs won the World Series in 2016, ending a drought of how many years?

    A. 106
    B. 107
    C. 108
    D. 109

CHAPTER 25 ANSWERS:

1. C. 15. Detroit defeated St. Louis 10-5 in the series.
2. C. 1903. The Boston Americans defeated the Pittsburgh Pirates 5-3 in the series.
3. A. World's Championship Series. It was not called the "World Series" until the 1930s.
4. B. Cincinnati Reds. It became known as the "Black Sox Scandal."
5. B. Two. It was the beginning of a dynastic run.
6. B. 1921. The Yankees lost to the Giants that year.
7. D. 1949. The Yankees beat the Dodgers that year.
8. A. Boston Red Sox. The home run came in the 12th inning of Game 6.
9. B. Pittsburgh Pirates. Though, they did win the title in 1971 and 1979.
10. C. 1976. It was only used every other year until 1986.
11. A. Kansas City Royals. Don Denkinger is remembered for the controversial call.
12. B. Boston Red Sox. The Curse of the Bambino continued.
13. A. Minnesota Twins. They defeated the Cardinals in 1987.
14. D. Oakland Athletics. The Dodgers won the Series in five games.
15. C. Five. The Twins beat the Braves in what many consider to be the best World Series of all time.
16. A. 1992. The Toronto Blue Jays won the World Series two years in a row.
17. True. They were consistently inconsistent.
18. C. 108. They defeated the Cleveland Indians in seven games.

DID YOU KNOW?

Home-field advantage in the World Series was not awarded to the team with the best regular season record until 2017.

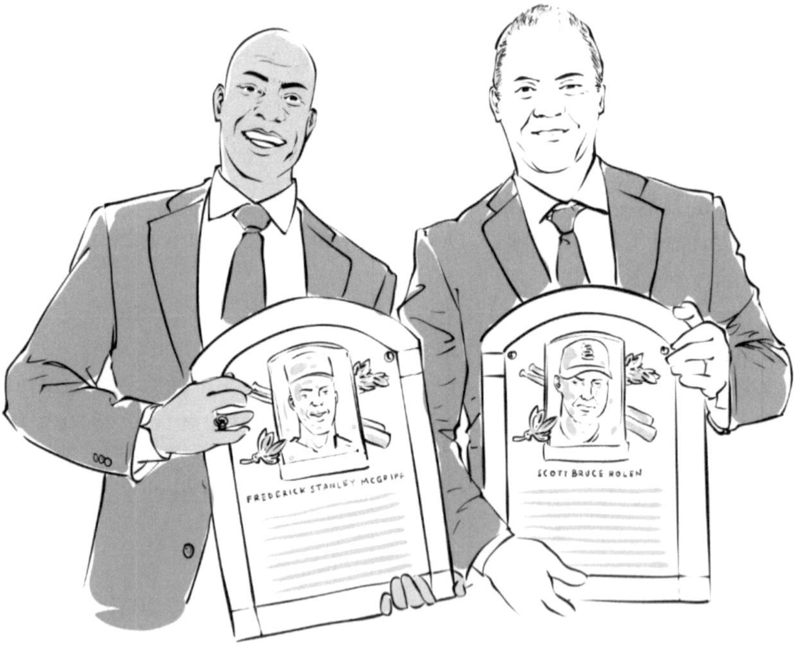
FREDERICK STANLEY MCGRIFF
SCOTT BRUCE ROLEN

CHAPTER 26:

BASEBALL HALL OF FAME

1. Stephen Carlton Clark established the Hall of Fame in 1939. He was the heir of which popular product of the time?

    A. Nestle chocolate
    B. Singer Sewing Machine
    C. Crunch bar
    D. The Tonette

2. Though the Hall was established in 1939, what year was the first group of players selected?

    A. 1934
    B. 1935
    C. 1936
    D. 1937

3. True or False: There is only one woman in the National Baseball Hall of Fame.

4. True or False: Lou Gehrig was the only player on the ballot when he was selected for the Hall of Fame.

5. Pete Rose is on the "permanently ineligible" list for the Hall of Fame because of what?

    A. Gambling
    B. Pine tar
    C. Corking bats
    D. Felony conviction

6. True or False: Until 2001, players were not able to pick which of their teams were depicted on their plaque in the Hall of Fame.

7. The United States Mint produced special coins to benefit the Hall of Fame in what year?

    A. 2010

B. 2011
C. 2012
D. 2013

8. Of the first five players inducted into the Hall of Fame, which one received the highest vote percentage?

   A. Ty Cobb
   B. Walter Johnson
   C. Babe Ruth
   D. Honus Wagner

9. Of the group selected in 1955, how many were from the Chicago White Sox?

   A. One
   B. Two
   C. Three
   D. Four

10. True or False: Jackie Robinson earned 82% of the vote in 1962 to gain entry.

11. Mickey Mantle was selected in his first year of eligibility. What year was that?

    A. 1974
    B. 1975
    C. 1976
    D. 1977

12. True or False: Duke Snider was selected in his first year of eligibility.

13. Hank Aaron was selected in 1982 along with which Cincinnati Reds player?

    A. Warren Giles
    B. Edd Roush
    C. Frank Robinson
    D. Eppa Rixey

14. Only one individual was selected in 1988. Who was it?

    A. Catfish Hunter
    B. Billy Williams

C. Johnny Bench
   D. Willie Stargell

15. True or False: Three pitchers and two umpires were selected in 1992.

16. Which of these Atlanta Braves was not selected in 2014?
    A. Bobby Cox
    B. Tom Glavine
    C. Greg Maddux
    D. John Smoltz

17. True or False: David Ortiz was the only 2022 selection who was in his first year of eligibility.

18. True or False: Joe Mauer and Adrian Beltre were both selected in 2024.

CHAPTER 26 ANSWERS:

1. B. Singer Sewing Machine.
2. C. 1936. Five were selected that first year.
3. True. Effa Manley, co-owner of the Newark Eagles of the Negro National League, was posthumously inducted into the Hall of Fame in 2006.
4. True. A special election was held as Gehrig was terminally ill at the time.
5. A. Gambling. He allegedly gambled while he was the Reds' manager in the 1980s.
6. False. The Hall allowed players to choose until 2001.
7. C. 2012. Although, they were not released until 2014.
8. A. Ty Cobb. He received over 98% of the vote.
9. B. Two. Ted Lyons and Ray Schalk both went to the Hall in 1955.
10. False. He only received 77.5% of the vote.
11. A. 1974. He received 88.22% of the vote.
12. False. He was selected in 1980.
13. C. Frank Robinson. They were both in their first year of eligibility.
14. D. Willie Stargell. He played 21 years for the Pirates.
15. False. Three pitchers and one umpire were selected that year.
16. D. John Smoltz. He was selected in 2015.
17. True. Four other players were selected that year, but none were in their first year of eligibility.
18. True. They were both in their first year of eligibility.

DID YOU KNOW?

Thirty-seven Negro League and Black baseball figures have been inducted into the Hall of Fame.

CHAPTER 27:
HOME RUN KINGS

1. Which player leads the all-time home run list?

    A. Hank Aaron
    B. Barry Bonds
    C. Babe Ruth
    D. Albert Pujols

2. Out of the top ten home run leaders, how many are in the Hall of Fame, as of 2024?

    A. Four
    B. Five
    C. Six
    D. Seven

3. True or False: Alex Rodriguez hit more home runs than Albert Pujols.

4. Barry Bonds also holds the single-season home run record. How many homers did he hit?

    A. 71
    B. 72
    C. 73
    D. 74

5. Which MLB player has hit 50 home runs with the fewest plate appearances?

    A. Jim Thome
    B. Babe Ruth
    C. Albert Belle
    D. Willie Mays

6. Who is the youngest player to hit 50 home runs in a season?

    A. Willie Mays

B. Ralph Kiner
   C. Prince Fielder
   D. Pete Alonso

7. Three out of the top six single-season home run performances belong to which player?

   A. Mark McGwire
   B. Sammy Sosa
   C. Barry Bonds
   D. Aaron Judge

8. True or False: Willie McCovey, Frank Thomas, and Ted Williams all hit 521 home runs in their careers.

9. True or False: Sammy Sosa is the only player in the top ten for career home runs who did not play 20 seasons.

10. As of the beginning of the 2024 season, which active player had the most home runs?

    A. Mike Trout
    B. Joey Votto
    C. Evan Longoria
    D. Giancarlo Stanton

11. Though Barry Bonds is atop the career home run list, he only led the league in home runs for how many seasons?

    A. One
    B. Two
    C. Three
    D. Four

12. True or False: Babe Ruth led the league in career home runs from 1921 to 1973.

13. True or False: Ed Williamson held the single season record for home runs before Babe Ruth.

14. True or False: Ralph Kiner and Johnny Mize tied as league leaders in home runs two years in a row.

15. True or False: Roger Maris took the single-season home run record in 1951.

16. True or False: Mark McGwire led the league in home runs four years in a row, the first player to do it since 1951.

17. True or False: Raphael Palmeiro hit more home runs in his career than David Ortiz.

18. True or False: The last time the league leader in home runs hit less than ten home runs on the season was in 1902.

CHAPTER 27 ANSWERS:

1. B. Barry Bonds. He hit 762 home runs in his career.
2. C. Six. The other four are ranked first, fourth, fifth, and ninth.
3. False. Pujols hit seven more home runs than Rodriguez.
4. C. 73. He hit those home runs in 2001.
5. A. Jim Thome. He hit 52 home runs with 613 plate appearances.
6. C. Prince Fielder. He was 23.
7. B. Sammy Sosa. He owns the third, fifth, and sixth spots on the single-season home run list.
8. True. McCovey needed the fewest plate appearances.
9. True. He played 18 seasons.
10. D. Giancarlo Stanton. He hit 402 home runs through the 2023 season.
11. B. 2. He led the league in 1993 and 2001.
12. True. It was his record until Hank Aaron took it.
13. True. Ruth claimed the record in 1919.
14. True. They tied in 1947 and 1948.
15. False. He took the record in 1961.
16. True. Ralph Kiner was the last player to do it before McGwire.
17. True. He hit 569 to Ortiz's 541.
18. False. Ty Cobb led the league in home runs during the 1909 season with nine.

DID YOU KNOW?

Giancarlo Stanton hit 59 home runs in 2017, and Aaron Judge hit 62 in 2022.

Rawlings
GOLD GLOVE AWARD
Rawlings
GOLD GLOVE AWARD
Rawlings
EST. 1887
Rawlings
Rawlings
PRESENTED ANNUALLY
TO EACH OF THE EIGHTEEN PLAYERS HONORING THEIR SELECTION AS
THE FINEST IN THE FIELD

CHAPTER 28:
GOLDEN GLOVES

1. Since its inception in the 1950s, Gold Glove awards have been sponsored by what company?

   A. Wilson
   B. Rawlings
   C. All-Star
   D. Easton

2. For the first few seasons, Gold Gloves were only awarded to which players?

   A. Infielders
   B. Outfielders
   C. Pitchers
   D. Catchers

3. True or False: Three centerfielders can win Gold Gloves in the same season.

4. Which player has won more Gold Gloves than anyone else in league history?

   A. Greg Maddux
   B. Brooks Robinson
   C. Jim Kaal
   D. Ivan Rodriguez

5. Which Gold Glove winner in 1999 caused controversy and caused many to question the prestige of the award?

   A. Roberto Alomar
   B. Ozzie Smith
   C. Derek Jeter
   D. Rafael Palmeiro

6. True or False: Ozzie Smith won 13 Gold Gloves at shortstop.

7. True or False: Brooks Robinson has won the most Gold Gloves at third base, with 14.

8. True or False: The first set of Gold Gloves was only awarded to nine players irrespective of their league.

9. Bobby Shantz won the first four Gold Gloves playing which position in the American League?
   A. Catcher
   B. First base
   C. Pitcher
   D. Shortstop

10. True or False: Vic Power won the first seven AL Gold Gloves at First Base, not counting the very first Gold Glove to both leagues.

11. Which player has the longest streak of Gold Glove awards?
    A. Brooks Robinson
    B. Earl Battey
    C. Jim Kaat
    D. Mark Belanger

12. Roberto Clemente is tied with which player for the most Gold Gloves as an outfielder?
    A. Curt Flood
    B. Willie Mays
    C. Al Kaline
    D. Andre Dawson

13. True or False: Roberto Alomar has won the most Gold Gloves at First Base.

14. Greg Maddux has the most Gold Gloves as a pitcher. Who has the second most?
    A. Bob Gibson
    B. Bobby Shantz
    C. Phil Nierko
    D. Jim Kaat

15. True or False: Ken Griffey Jr. has more Gold Gloves than Omar Vizquel.

16. Cal Ripken Jr had a long career, but only how many Gold Gloves?

A. Zero
B. One
C. Two
D. Three

17. Which of these players have not won Gold Gloves in multiple positions?

    A. Darin Erstad
    B. DJ LeMahieu
    C. Placido Polanco
    D. Mike Matheny

18. True or False: Evan Longoria and Joe Mauer both have three Gold Gloves.

CHAPTER 28 ANSWERS:

1. B. Rawlings. The company also makes MLB baseballs.
2. B. Outfielders. Other players weren't recognized until 1961.
3. True. The award does not distinguish between outfield positions.
4. A. Greg Maddux. He won 18 of the awards, including 13 in a row.
5. D. Rafael Palmeiro. He only played 28 games at first base that season.
6. True. That number is tied for fourth highest among all winners.
7. False. Robinson won 16 of the awards, most among third basemen.
8. True. Every other year, a set of nine has been awarded to each league.
9. C. Pitcher. That included the first Gold Glove, meaning he won it over National League pitchers.
10. True. It was the longest opening streak for the award but not the longest streak of all time.
11. A. Brooks Robinson. He won 16 in a row.
12. B. Willie Mays. They both won 12 awards.
13. False. Alomar has the most awards at Second Base.
14. D. Jim Kaat. He collected 16 to Maddux's 18.
15. False. Vizquel has 11 to Griffey's ten.
16. C. 2. Not many for a great career.
17. D. Mike Matheny. He only won as a catcher.
18. True. Mauer as a catcher, Longoria as a third baseman.

DID YOU KNOW?

Utility players only became eligible for Gold Glove Awards in 2022.

CY YOUNG AWARD
PRESENTED TO
THE OUTSTANDING
AMERICAN LEAGUE PITCHER

CHAPTER 29:
CY YOUNG AWARD WINNERS

1. Which Baseball Commissioner introduced the Cy Young Award in 1956?

   A. Happy Chandler
   B. Ford Frick
   C. William Eckert
   D. Bowie Kuhn

2. As of 2010, how many places does each voter get to select for the award?

   A. Two
   B. Three
   C. Four
   D. Five

3. Before 1970, how many places did each voter get to select for the award?

   A. Zero
   B. One
   C. Two
   D. Three

4. True or False: William Eckert was the Commissioner who began giving the Cy Young Award to one pitcher from each league.

5. Who was the first pitcher to win the Cy Young Award?

   A. Warren Spahn
   B. Bob Turley
   C. Don Newcombe
   D. Early Wynn

6. Who has won the most Cy Young Awards?

   A. Randy Johnson

B. Roger Clemens
   C. Steve Carlton
   D. Greg Maddux

7. Who was the first modern closer to win the Cy Young Award?

   A. Dennis Eckersley
   B. Eric Gagne
   C. Mariano Rivera
   D. Shane Bieber

8. True or False: Roger Clemens won his seven awards with four different teams.

9. Which pitcher won the Cy Young with more than 30 wins on the season?

   A. Denny McLain
   B. Bob Welch
   C. Catfish Hunter
   D. Ron Guidry

10. Which Cy Young pitcher's winning season had the most strikeouts?

    A. Steve Carlton
    B. Pedro Martinez
    C. Vida Blue
    D. Randy Johnson

11. True or False: Bob Gibson had the lowest ERA of any Cy Young winner.

12. True or False: Greg Maddux has more Cy Young Awards than Randy Johnson.

13. Which of these players did not win three Cy Young Awards?

    A. Jim Palmer
    B. Max Scherzer
    C. Roy Halladay
    D. Justin Verlander

14. Roger Clemens' first and last awards are separated by how many years?

    A. 15
    B. 16

C. 17
D. 18

15. True or False: Gaylord Perry won the 1972 AL Cy Young with a 24-16 record.

16. True or False: Perry is the oldest player to win the Cy Young, at 40 years old.

17. True or False: Dwight Gooden is the youngest player to win the award at 21 years old.

18. True or False: The first knuckleball pitcher to win the Cy Young was R.A. Dickey in 2010.

CHAPTER 29 ANSWERS:

1. B. Ford Frick. The award was only given to one pitcher until Frick retired.
2. D. Five. A weighted sum is used to determine the winner.
3. B. One. Each vote was one point, and the most votes won.
4. True. The change was in response to fan feedback.
5. C. Don Newcombe. He had 27 wins and 139 strikeouts that season.
6. B. Roger Clemens. He has seven of them.
7. A. Dennis Eckersley. He won the award in 1992.
8. True. He won with the Astros, Blue Jays, Red Sox, and Yankees.
9. A. Denny McLain. He had 31 wins in 1968.
10. D. Randy Johnson. His 1999 season included 313 strikeouts.
11. True. His 1968 season featured a 1.12 ERA in 31 games.
12. False. Johnson had five to Maddux's four.
13. C. Roy Halladay. He only has two.
14. D. 18. 1986 to 2004.
15. True. His ERA was 1.92.
16. False. Clemens won one at age 42.
17. False. He was only 20 years old!
18. False. He won in 2012.

DID YOU KNOW?

Sandy Koufax was the first pitcher to win the award with a unanimous vote, in 1963.

CHAPTER 30:

UNBEATABLE RECORDS

1. Ichiro Suzuki has the record for the base hits in a single season. How many hits?

   A. 246
   B. 254
   C. 262
   D. 270

2. True or False: George Sisler got 257 hits, five less than Suzuki's record, on 70 fewer at-bats.

3. Which player holds the sad record of playing the most games without reaching the playoffs?

   A. Ernie Banks
   B. Luke Appling
   C. Mickey Vernon
   D. Buddy Bell

4. Nolan Ryan has the most strikeouts in the history of the sport. How many?

   A. 4,875
   B. 5,218
   C. 5,524
   D. 5,714

5. True or False: Second place on the strikeout list is Randy Johnson, with 4,875.

6. After playing for 27 years, it is no surprise that Nolan Ryan leads in which category?

   A. Cy Young Awards
   B. Hit by pitch
   C. Base on balls
   D. Wild pitches

7. True or False: Rickey Henderson stole 140 bases in 1982.

8. Rickey Henderson also holds the record for the most bases stolen over a career. Who is second?

   A. Lou Brock
   B. Billy Hamilton
   C. Ty Cobb
   D. Tim Raines

9. Hack Wilson set which record in 1930, likely never to be broken?

   A. Plate appearances in a season
   B. RBIs in a season
   C. Doubles in a season
   D. Cycles in a season

10. In a record that still stands today, Owen Wilson hit how many triples in 1912?

    A. 32
    B. 36
    C. 40
    D. 44

11. True or False: Barry Bonds holds the top three spots in bases on balls throughout a season.

12. True or False: Babe Ruth holds the modern baseball record for runs scored in a season with 221.

13. Pete Rose holds two unbreakable records. First, how many plate appearances did he collect throughout his career?

    A. 13,992
    B. 14,285
    C. 15,367
    D. 15,890

14. True or False: Pete Rose also holds the career hits record with 4,256.

15. True or False: Hank Aaron holds the MLB record for total bases with 6,856.

16. Ron Hunt got hit by how many pitches in 1971, and no one has been close since?

A. 44
B. 50
C. 54
D. 60

17. True or False: Grover Alexander holds the MLB record for shutouts in a season with 16.

18. True or False: Joe DiMaggio holds the MLB record with hits in 56 straight games.

CHAPTER 30 ANSWERS:

1. C. 262. Most of the other players in the top ten played before 1930.
2. True.
3. A. Ernie Banks. He played 2,528 games in 19 seasons.
4. D. 5714. He gathered those over a total of 27 seasons in the league.
5. True. He played 22 seasons.
6. C. Base on balls. Ryan has 2,795 walks.
7. False. Henderson stole 130 bases in 1982, a modern baseball record.
8. A. Lou Brock. His 938 is well behind Henderson's 1,406.
9. B. RBIs in a season. He hit 191.
10. B. 36. The closest modern player was Curtis Granderson, who hit 23 in 2007.
11. True. He had 232, 198, and 177 in 2004, 2002, and 2001, respectively.
12. False. He holds the record, but it is only 177 runs scored in 1921.
13. D. 15,890. He collected them over 24 years.
14. True. His career was long and prosperous.
15. True. The next closest player is Albert Pujols, with 6,211.
16. B. 50. Ty France notched 34 in 2023.
17. True. Bob Gibson got 13 in 1968.
18. True. No one has gotten to within ten games of that record.

DID YOU KNOW?

The 1906 Cubs and 2001 Mariners have both won 116 games in a season, tied for the record.

CHAPTER 31:
THE BIGGEST MOMENTS

1. True or False: Jackie Robinson played his first game for the Brooklyn Dodgers in 1947, several years before the Civil Rights Movement.

2. Babe Ruth's contract was sold by the Red Sox to the Yankees in what year?
   A. 1918
   B. 1919
   C. 1920
   D. 1921

3. Hank Aaron passed Babe Ruth's home run record in what year?
   A. 1966
   B. 1974
   C. 1979
   D. 1980

4. The Shot Heard 'Round the World in 1951 helped the Giants beat the Dodgers to win the NL pennant. Who hit the home run?
   A. Bobby Thomson
   B. Hank Aaron
   C. Joe DiMaggio
   D. Ty Cobb

5. True or False: The only walk-off home run in Game 7 of the World Series took place in 1960.

6. True or False: Lou Gehrig was the first player to have his number retired by his team.

7. Roger Maris topped Babe Ruth's single-season home run record with how many in 1961?
   A. 60

B. 61
C. 62
D. 63

8. True or False: Tommy John underwent the surgery now named after him and then went on to pitch until he was 45 years old.

9. On September 6, 1995, Cal Ripken Jr passed which player for the most consecutive games played all time?

   A. Hank Aaron
   B. Joe DiMaggio
   C. Ty Cobb
   D. Lou Gehrig

10. This journeyman pitcher threw the only perfect game in World Series history.

    A. Don Larsen
    B. Sal Maglie
    C. Whitey Ford
    D. Tom Morgan

11. True or False: Carlton Fisk won Game 6 of the 1975 World Series, helping the Red Sox break their curse.

12. True or False: Reggie Jackson hit three home runs in Game 6 of the 1977 World Series, bringing the title to the Yankees.

13. Pete Rose passed this player with his 4,193rd hit.

    A. Lou Gehrig
    B. Hank Aaron
    C. Ty Cobb
    D. Willie Mays

14. True or False: The first MLB All-Star Game took place alongside the World's Fair.

15. An error by which Boston Red Sox player in the 1986 World Series became infamous?

    A. Calvin Schiraldi
    B. Bob Stanley
    C. Rich Gedman
    D. Bill Buckner

16. *Sports Illustrated* published an infamous story about steroids in which year?

    A. 2001
    B. 2002
    C. 2003
    D. 2004

17. True or False: Mark McGwire passed Roger Maris before Bonds passed him three years later.

18. True or False: The MLB initially dropped the investigation against Pete Rose's gambling allegation but reopened it days later and discovered the truth.

CHAPTER 31 ANSWERS:

1. True. He debuted in front of 26,623 fans.
2. C. 1920. He added to "Murderer's Row," winning four titles in ten years.
3. B. 1974. His 715th home run came on April 8, 1974.
4. A. Bobby Thomson. It broke a tie between the two teams for the NL crown.
5. True. The Pirates defeated the Yankees.
6. True. He passed away two years later from the disease now named after him.
7. B. 61. He hit his final home run in the last game of the season.
8. False. He pitched until he was 46.
9. D. Lou Gehrig. The ovation for Ripken lasted 22 minutes.
10. A. Don Larsen. He helped the Yankees beat the Dodgers.
11. False. The Sox won Game 6 but lost to the Reds in Game 7.
12. True. The performance helped Jackson earn the nickname, "Mr. October."
13. C. Ty Cobb. The record was broken in 1985.
14. True. The league did not think it would become a tradition.
15. D. The ball rolling between his legs is a well-known baseball moment.
16. B. 2002. The scandal caused an upheaval in the sport.
17. True. The home run race of 1998 was a popular moment in the sport.
18. True. Rose perhaps nearly escaped punishment from the league.

DID YOU KNOW?

Some players argue that Babe Ruth did not call his shot during the famous home run in 1932.

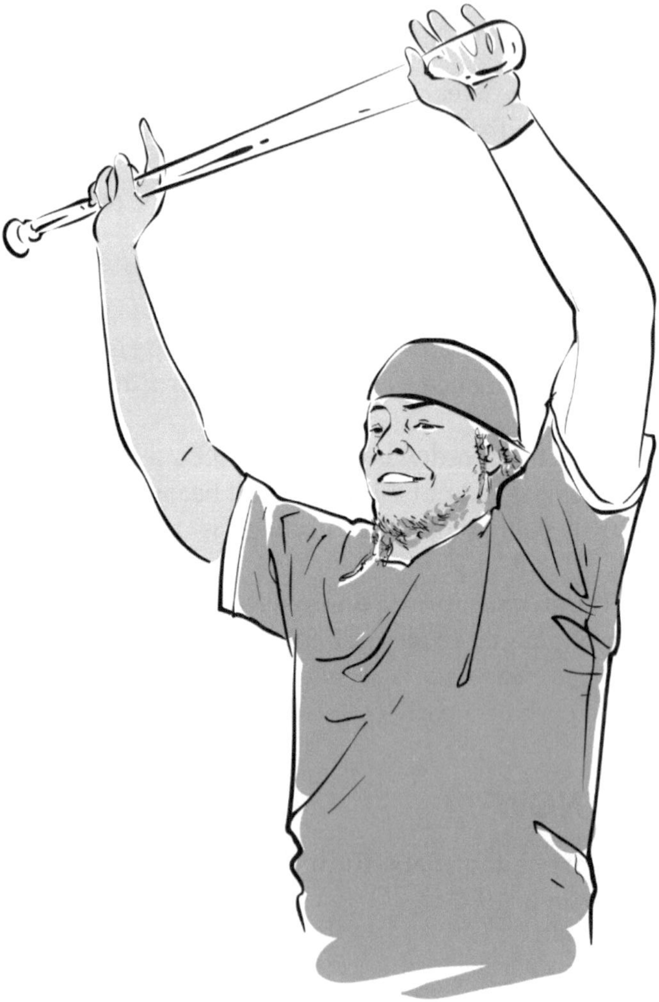

CHAPTER 32:
THE ALL-STAR GAME

1. True or False: The All-Star Game is also known as the "Midsummer Classic."

2. True or False: There were no All-Star Games in 1945 and 2020.

3. From 1959 to 1962, there were how many All-Star Games per season?

   A. Zero
   B. One
   C. Two
   D. Three

4. Beginning in 1982, how many players were named to each roster for the All-Star Game?

   A. 28
   B. 30
   C. 32
   D. 34

5. True or False: The National League wore custom uniforms during the very first All-Star Game.

6. True or False: The 2014 All-Star Game was the first to feature custom socks.

7. Who was the first player selected to an All-Star team by write-in votes?

   A. Rico Carty
   B. Steve Garvey
   C. Robin Ventura
   D. Eric Chavez

8. In 1957, how many Cincinnati Reds made the All-Star starting roster?

A. Four
   B. Five
   C. Six
   D. Seven

9. True or False: Terry Steinbach was the 1988 All-Star Game MVP after accusations of Oakland's fans electing him unfairly.

10. True or False: The MLB canceled 65 million fraudulent votes during the 2015 All-Star Game voting.

11. Which was the first year a designated hitter was allowed to be used in the All-Star Game?
    A. 1981
    B. 1989
    C. 1992
    D. 1995

12. The All-Star MVP Award was originally called what?
    A. Arch Ward Memorial Award
    B. Commissioner's Trophy
    C. The Ted Williams Most Valuable Player Award
    D. The Ty Cobb Award

13. True or False: The first All-Star MVP Award was in 1962, and it was awarded to two different players at the two All-Star Games.

14. True or False: The first Hall of Fame player to win the All-Star MVP was Willie Mays in 1968.

15. Which of these players has not won two All-Star MVPs?
    A. Mike Trout
    B. Cal Ripken Jr.
    C. Willie Mays
    D. Derek Jeter

16. Only six players have won the All-Star MVP during their only All-Star appearance. Which of these is one of them?
    A. Miguel Tejada
    B. Prince Fielder
    C. Bo Jackson
    D. Mariano Rivera

17. True or False: The St. Louis Cardinals have never had an All-Star MVP.

18. True or False: Derek Jeter is the only player to win All-Star MVP and World Series MVP in the same season.

CHAPTER 32 ANSWERS:

1. True. The game usually occurs around the halfway point of the season.
2. True. World War II and the Covid-19 pandemic canceled those games.
3. C. Two. The extra game was played to raise more money for the players' pension fund.
4. B. 30. It has since increased to 34.
5. True. The NL conformed to players wearing their own team's uniforms during the game after the first iteration.
6. False. It was the first to feature custom caps, not socks.
7. A. Rico Carty. He was selected in 1970.
8. D. Seven. Cincinnati fans had overwhelmed the voting process.
9. True. His performance spoke for itself.
10. True. The votes would have elected eight Royals to start in the game.
11. B. 1989. It was only allowed if the game was played in an AL ballpark, until 2010.
12. A. Arch Ward Memorial Trophy. It has had many names over the years.
13. True. Leon Wagner and Maury Willis were the first recipients.
14. False. Mays won the All-Star MVP in 1963.
15. D. Derek Jeter. He only won it once, in 2000.
16. C. Bo Jackson. He won the 1989 All-Star MVP, in his only All-Star appearance.
17. True. The Cardinals are the only franchise to not have an All-Star MVP.
18. True. He won them both in 2000.

DID YOU KNOW?

The 2023 All-Star MVP was Elias Diaz.

CHAPTER 33:
SCANDALS & HEADLINES

1. True or False: The 2022 season was the first year for Cleveland to have the Guardians name.

2. True or False: Aaron Judge won the 2022 AL MVP, and the Yankees won the AL Pennant.

3. The 2023 season was the first year that pitchers had to pay attention to what?

   A. Pitch Timer
   B. Designated hitter
   C. Switch hitting
   D. Steal leads

4. The 2023 season also restricted which defensive strategy?

   A. Intentional walks
   B. Defensive shifts
   C. Knuckleballs
   D. Multiple relief pitchers

5. True or False: In the 2023 season, the size of the bases increased from 14 to 20 inches.

6. True or False: The 2023 season introduced a rule in extra innings that see the team on offense start with a runner on first base.

7. The day before Jackie Robinson made his debut, the Dodgers manager, Leo Durocher, was suspended for how long?

   A. 20 games
   B. 40 games
   C. 100 games
   D. One year

8. George Steinbrenner was suspended for 15 months in 1990 because he paid a confessed gambler to dig up dirt on which Yankees player?

   A. Deion Sanders
   B. Don Mattingly
   C. Dave Winfield
   D. Mel Hall

9. True or False: The St. Louis Cardinals were caught stealing signs during the 2017 playoffs.

10. True or False: In 2007, a U.S. senator released a 400-page report that implicated 30 players in a steroid scandal.

11. The 2017 Houston Astros were caught using many techniques to steal signs. Which of these is not one of them?

    A. Center field camera
    B. Smartphones in dugout
    C. Trash can noise
    D. Watching opponents practice

12. Which MLB team was caught up in a cocaine scandal during the 1985 season?

    A. New York Mets
    B. Houston Astros
    C. Texas Rangers
    D. Pittsburgh Pirates

13. True or False: In 2013, 20 players were accused of using HGH in connection with a clinic named Biogenesis of America.

14. True or False: A substance called Scorpion Tack became a scandal in 2021 as pitchers were using it to doctor baseballs.

15. Which baseball commissioner was responsible for banning the most players during his tenure?

    A. William Eckert
    B. Kenesaw Mountain Landis
    C. Happy Chandler
    D. Ford Frick

16. True or False: Benny Kauff was banned in 1921 for selling stolen cars.

17. True or False: When Heinie Groh tried to hold out for a better contract in 1921, he was threatened to either play or be banned.

18. True or False: Willie Mays and Mickey Mantle were banned in 1980 for working with casinos in New Jersey. They were reinstated ten years later.

CHAPTER 33 ANSWERS:

1. True. The name was switched from the Indians.
2. False. Judge won the MVP, but the Yankees lost to the Astros in the ALCS.
3. A. Pitch Timer. A pitch violation would be ruled an automatic ball.
4. B. Defensive shifts. The change was an effort to increase scoring.
5. False. The bases increased from 15 to 18 inches.
6. False. The runner starts on second base.
7. D. One year. The manager had been around too much gambling.
8. C. Dave Winfield. The suspension was two years, then reduced to 15 months.
9. False. The Houston Astros were caught stealing signs during the 2017 World Series.
10. False. About 90 players were named in the report.
11. D. Watching opponents practice. The scandal was quite extensive.
12. D. Pittsburgh Pirates. The Pittsburgh Drug Trials made national news.
13. True. It was the most players ever suspended at the same time.
14. False. The substance was called Spider Tack.
15. B. Kenesaw Mountain Landis. The Black Sox scandal helped boost his numbers.
16. True. Though, Kauff was acquitted of all charges in court.
17. True. He elected to play.
18. False. They were reinstated in 1985, ten years before Mantle's passing in 1995.

DID YOU KNOW?

Pete Rose was placed on the ineligible list on August 24, 1989.

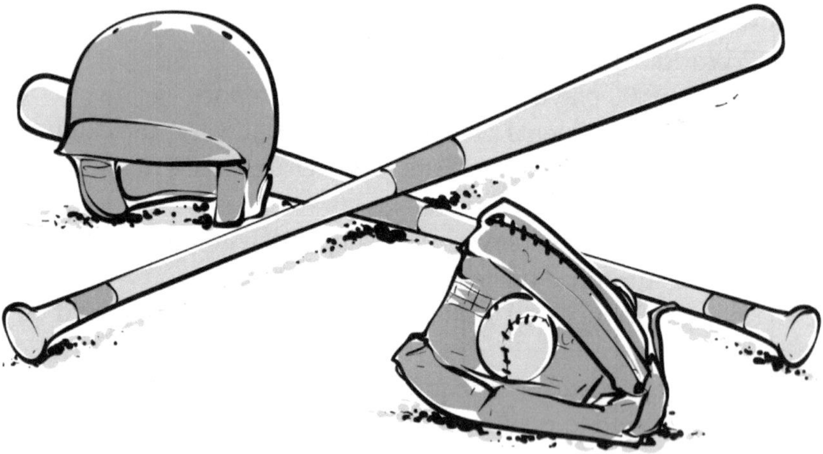

CHAPTER 34:
STATISTICS & ACRONYMS

1. AO. Different from a ground-out.
2. BB. It takes at least four pitches.
3. CG. A pitcher needs endurance for this.
4. ERA. A pitcher wants this number to be low.
5. IRA. Relievers can blame some of these on the starter.
6. IPS. How long do these starting pitchers last?
7. SVO. A closer only gets so many chances.
8. WP. Are these the pitcher's fault, or the catcher's?
9. PK. Don't let them lead off or steal.
10. SBR. Points a runner scores by robbery.
11. LOB. This number should be low if you want your RBIs to be high.
12. GIDP. It is a quick way to end an inning.
13. CS. A runner does not want this to happen.
14. IBB. Pitchers use this when they do not want to face a hitter.
15. CGL. A pitcher needs a lot of stamina, but if they don't get help, they only get one of these.
16. MB9. This represents how many runners a pitcher allows.
17. TB. How far does a batter travel?
18. GRSL. It is the biggest play in baseball.

CHAPTER 34 ANSWERS:

1. Fly Outs (Air). This is a good stat for pitchers and fielders; not so much for batters.
2. Base on Balls (Walk). Batters love these but maybe not as much as hits.
3. Complete Game. It's a show of skill and endurance.
4. Earned Run Average. A low number represents dominance on the mound.
5. Inherited Runs Allowed. A reliever isn't always to blame.
6. Innings Per Start. More innings likely make a pitcher more valuable.
7. Save Opportunities. Closers should get a lot of saves but not waste too many chances.
8. Wild Pitches. It's a costly mistake between the pitcher and catcher.
9. Pickoffs. A quick defense can stop a fast runner.
10. Stolen Base Runs. Stealing can lead to scoring.
11. Left on Base. Stranded runners can frustrate an offense.
12. Ground into Double Plays. Great defensive plays aided by a pitcher.
13. Caught Stealing. It's a bad stat for runners who want to score sooner.
14. Intentional Bases on Balls. Barry Bonds holds the record for these.
15. Complete Game Losses. Sometimes, a pitcher throws a great game but still loses.
16. Baserunners Per 9 Innings. If a pitcher lets too many players on base, in any fashion, it's not a good thing.
17. Total Bases. It represents how much offense a player has created.
18. Grand Slams. The biggest players make the biggest plays.

DID YOU KNOW?

Statcast was installed in all 30 stadiums in 2015 to better track ball speed, spin, and other data.

CONCLUSION

So, there you have it. More than 600 difficult questions that cover more than a hundred years of baseball. From the sport's humble beginnings all the way to today's game, there are questions and Answers: for every topic in between.

When a sport has lasted as long as baseball, there must be a good reason. One of those reasons is the quality of players that have come through and contributed to the game. The sport is full of good people making great choices, and their actions have paved the way for baseball to continue its success all over the world.

The biggest names in the sport made big impacts, but some of those smaller stories also deserve attention, so be sure to check out every chapter of the book, even if you are not familiar with some of the topics covered.

Besides, the more you explore these chapters, the easier it will be to unleash your newfound knowledge on all of your fellow baseball fans. Whether it is an unknown statistical acronym, or which players from decades past were putting up impressive numbers, there is plenty to examine and discover.

Most importantly, it can be difficult to remember how the game has changed over the years. Young baseball fans in the 2030s will not remember what it was like to play without a pitch clock, and fans today don't remember what it was like not to have more than two teams in the postseason. Way back when, a team only had to finish at the top of the regular season standings to win the pennant. It's a very different sport today, and it'll be different 30 years from now.

These differences are apparent when one examines some of those unbreakable records. They are unbreakable because the sport is played differently, and competition is much fiercer than it was 100 years ago.

Hopefully, you enjoyed this book and showed your competitive spirit when trying to figure out all the right Answers:.

Baseball is a beautiful game, and everyone who has been part of it should be celebrated for contributing to such a wonderful piece of American history.

Keep swinging for the fences!